THE STATES AND
PRIVATE
HIGHER EDUCATION

Problems and Policies
in a New Era

A REPORT OF THE CARNEGIE COUNCIL
ON POLICY STUDIES IN HIGHER EDUCATION

*A report of the
Carnegie Council
on Policy Studies
in Higher Education*

THE STATES AND PRIVATE HIGHER EDUCATION

Problems and Policies
in a New Era

Jossey-Bass Publishers
San Francisco • Washington • London • 1977

THE STATES AND PRIVATE HIGHER EDUCATION
Problems and Policies in a New Era
The Carnegie Council on Policy Studies in Higher Education

Copyright © 1977 by: The Carnegie Foundation
for the Advancement of Teaching

Jossey-Bass, Inc., Publishers
615 Montgomery Street
San Francisco, California 94111

Jossey-Bass Limited
28 Banner Street
London EC1Y 8QE

This report is issued by the Carnegie Council on Policy Studies
in Higher Education with headquarters at 2150 Shattuck Avenue
Berkeley, California 94704.

Copies are available from Jossey-Bass, San Francisco,
for the United States, Canada, and Possessions.
Copies for the rest of the world available from
Jossey-Bass, London.

Library of Congress Catalogue Card Number LC 77-90848

International Standard Book Number ISBN 0-87589-363-5

Manufactured in the United States of America

DESIGN BY WILLI BAUM

FIRST EDITION

Code 7759

The Carnegie Council Series

Selective Admissions in Higher
Education: Comment and Recom-
mendations and Two Reports
*The Carnegie Council on Policy
Studies in Higher Education.
Winton H. Manning, Warren W.
Willingham, Hunter M. Breland,
and Associates*

Missions of the College Curriculum:
A Contemporary Review with Sug-
gestions
*The Carnegie Foundation for the
Advancement of Teaching*

Curriculum:
The American Undergraduate
Course of Study Since 1636
Frederick Rudolph

The States and Private
Higher Education: Problems
and Policies in a New Era
*The Carnegie Council on Policy
Studies in Higher Education*

*The following technical reports are available from the Carnegie
Council on Policy Studies in Higher Education, 2150 Shattuck Avenue,
Berkeley, California 94704.*

The States and Higher Education:
A Proud Past and a Vital Future
Supplement to a Commentary of
The Carnegie Foundation for the
Advancement of Teaching
*The Carnegie Foundation for
the Advancement of Teaching*

Changing Practices in
Undergraduate Education
*Robert Blackburn, Ellen
Armstrong, Clifton Conrad,
James Didham, Thomas McKune*

Aspects of American Higher
Education 1969-1975
Martin Trow

Contents

Preface

The Carnegie Council on Higher Education has had a continuing interest in the welfare of the private sector of higher education.

In *More Than Survival* (1975), we expressed concern for the "health of the private sector," spoke of it as "one of the main sources of strength" of higher education, and regretted that "the rules of the game are now too often unfair to the private sector."

In *The Federal Role in Postsecondary Education* (1975), we recommended an expansion of the State Student Incentive Grant (SSIG) program of the federal government and pioneered in proposing a federal program of tuition equalization grants.

In *Low or No Tuition* (1975a), we were concerned with the tuition gap between private and public institutions.

In *The States and Higher Education* (1976), we set forth, as one of our five major concerns, the preservation of the private sector. We noted its great contributions to diversity and to excellence.

This present report comes after the realization, in the early 1970s, that the financial situation of many private institutions of higher education was precarious and after early efforts of the states (and the federal government) to provide assistance. It precedes what will be the intensified problems of the 1980s and early 1990s. It seeks to present the situation as it now exists, to evaluate the programs undertaken to date, and to make recommendations for future action.

We are concerned here chiefly with the responsibilities of the states toward *undergraduate* education within nonprofit private universities, comprehensive institutions, and liberal arts colleges. Since graduate study and research activities within universities are national (or at least regional) in scope, and since many of the problems of financing them are more closely related to federal than to state policy, we do not focus here on these aspects of private research universities.[1] Also, in selecting our main emphasis, we do not wish to minimize the value of private two-year colleges and of specialized institutions; but they are highly diverse and it is difficult to generalize about them. We believe, moreover, that an environment that permits the four-year institutions, as a segment, to survive should have the same effect, in general, on two-year and specialized institutions (with the exception of those that serve primarily as seminaries and theological schools, which have very special constitutional problems in terms of public financial support).

The Carnegie Council recognizes the benefits provided society by the proprietary section of postsecondary education. But good, comprehensive data about these institutions are difficult to obtain, and the institutions are even more diverse in terms of programs and structures than those comprising the specialized nonprofit sector. The Council believes that the proprietary sector, which tends to have fewer controls over the establishment and the accreditation of institutions and a far less venerable tradition than the nonprofit sector, offers some very special problems in the receipt and supervision of public support; it is not our purpose to analyze these special problems here.

Concern over the future of private higher education led to the preparation in recent years of several other reports and studies relating wholly or in part to public policy toward private higher education. They include the volume of essays edited by David Breneman and Chester Finn of the Brookings Institution (forthcoming); a report by a special task force of the Education Commission of the States, chaired by Governor Otis R. Bowen of Indiana and summarized in Education Commission of the States (1977); the report by the Consortium on the Financing of Higher Education (1975); the report of the New Jersey Commission on Financing Post-Secondary Education (1976); and a report relating to the future of higher education in the South, issued by the Southern Regional Education Board (Spence, 1977).

---

[1] We refer the reader to Carnegie Council (1975c, Section 5) for a discussion of national policy vis-a-vis research universities.

A major difference between this report and other recent studies is that our report is based in part on the results of a study specifically designed to assess the impact of existing state policies toward private higher education on enrollments, finances, autonomy, academic freedom, and other conditions of private institutions. To the best of our knowledge, it is the only study of this type that has been conducted.

On the whole, the other recent reports, like our report, take a position generally favorable to improved federal and state student-aid policies as the major approach to public support of private higher education. But some of them differ from our report in the relative emphasis placed on student aid as opposed to various types of institutional aid and in a number of recommendations relating to student aid. In addition, several of these reports advocate increasing tuition in all or in some sectors of public higher education, whereas we believe that policies relating to tuition in public higher education should be determined on their own merits and not as a means of supporting private higher education.

This study benefited from the assistance of the presidents and their staffs in some 230 institutions who completed questionnaires on the impact of state measures to aid private institutions; from the site visits made by Dr. Peggy Heim to 28 institutions in five states; and from her extensive interviews with state government officials in California, Illinois, New York, Pennsylvania, and South Carolina. Those interviewed included legislators, staff assistants of major legislative committees dealing with higher education and with appropriations, state budget officers, the directors and staffs of coordinating councils of higher education, and the directors and staffs of state scholarship agencies. Also interviewed were executive heads of several state systems of higher education and the directors of state independent college associations. The institutions and individuals on whom she called were uniformly most cooperative and helpful. The Council is grateful to them all.

Several individuals provided special assistance: Joseph Boyd of the Illinois Scholarship Commission; Arthur Marmaduke of the California Scholarship Commission; Morgan Odell of the California Association of Independent Colleges and Universities; Donna Hunt, Director of Student Aid at Mills College; Wayne Weaver, Vice President of Finance at Furman University; and Theodore Drews,

United States Office of Education. To them we extend our special thanks.

The Council also wishes to acknowledge the advice given by Howard Bowen throughout the development of this report. His views on state support for private higher education are not identical with those of the Council, but his suggestions were always informed and wise.

The Council wishes particularly to express appreciation to Peggy Heim and Margaret S. Gordon, and to the following staff members who also assisted with this report: Charlotte Alhadeff, Matthew Chen, Patricia Fosler, Marian Gade, Ruth Goto, Sidney Hollister, Katherine Jako, Caroline Lawton, and Sandra Loris.

Members of the Carnegie Council on Policy Studies in Higher Education

Nolen M. Ellison
President
Cuyahoga Community College

E. K. Fretwell Jr.
President
State University of New York College at Buffalo

Philip R. Lee, M.D.
Professor of Social Medicine
and Director, Health Policy Program
University of California, San Francisco

Margaret L. A. MacVicar
Associate Professor of Physics
Massachusetts Institute of Technology

Rosemary Park
Professor of Education Emeritus
University of California, Los Angeles

James A. Perkins
Chairman of the Board
International Council for Educational Development

Alan Pifer
President
The Carnegie Foundation for the Advancement of Teaching

Joseph B. Platt
President
Claremont University Center

Lois D. Rice
Vice President
College Entrance Examination Board

William M. Roth
Trustee
Carnegie Institute, Washington, D.C.

Stephen H. Spurr
Professor
LBJ School of Public Affairs
University of Texas

Clark Kerr
Chairperson
Carnegie Council on Policy Studies in Higher Education

THE STATES AND PRIVATE HIGHER EDUCATION

Problems and Policies in a New Era

A REPORT OF THE CARNEGIE COUNCIL
ON POLICY STUDIES IN HIGHER EDUCATION

1

General Considerations

1. The private sector enrolls just over one-fifth of all students in higher education (Figure 1), offers a wide diversity of institutions for student choice, and includes a substantial proportion of high quality academic programs (Figure 2). It also saves the taxpayers almost $5 billion a year (net), the estimated cost to the states of absorbing its enrollments in public institutions.

2. In the late 1960s and early 1970s, this sector went through a difficult time (as did much of the larger public sector). Overall, the private sector in 1976–77 appears to be holding its own financially, but with great variations among institutions and with a possible reduction in the quality of some facilities and some programs. The current stability of the sector as a whole is due partly to self-help efforts by the private institutions and partly to increasing state and federal government responsiveness to the new need of the private sector for financial support.

About 40 states now have programs of direct or indirect assistance to the private sector and the federal government provides student aid and institutional support to both public and private institutions and their students. State support per student in private institutions now runs at a rate of about one-ninth (11 percent) of the support per student in public institutions (Table 1)[1]. Federal funds for student aid per FTE (full-time equivalent)[2] student in private institutions run about 40 to 50 percent above amounts per full-time equivalent (FTE) student in public institutions.

[1] Tables are found at the end of the report and near the point of first reference in each technical supplement.

[2] See the glossary of specialized terms used in this report, following Section 5.

Figure 1. Distribution of higher education enrollment and institutions
in the United States, private and public sectors, 1976

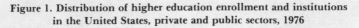

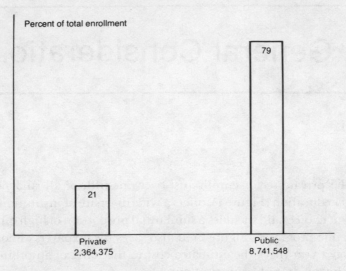

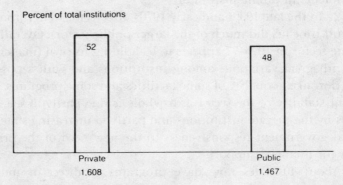

Sources: Enrollment: U.S. National Center for Education Statistics (1977c); Institutions: U.S. National Center for Education Statistics (1977b, Table 1).

**Figure 2. Contributions of private higher education to institutional diversity,
to student bodies and faculties of high academic ability, and
to high–quality graduate programs**

Diversity

Private as percent of total institutions
with specified characteristics

Institutions with enrollments
under 500 students 82

Institutions for women only 98

Institutions for men only 94

Institutions founded predominately
for Black students 66

Student bodies and faculties
of high academic ability

Institutions with combined
freshman SAT scores over 1000 73

Institutional affiliation of
members of National Academy
of Sciences, 1975 (°o of members,
not institutions) 63

High quality graduate programs

Private as percent of all programs

Top ranked graduate departments 58

Top ranked professional schools 57

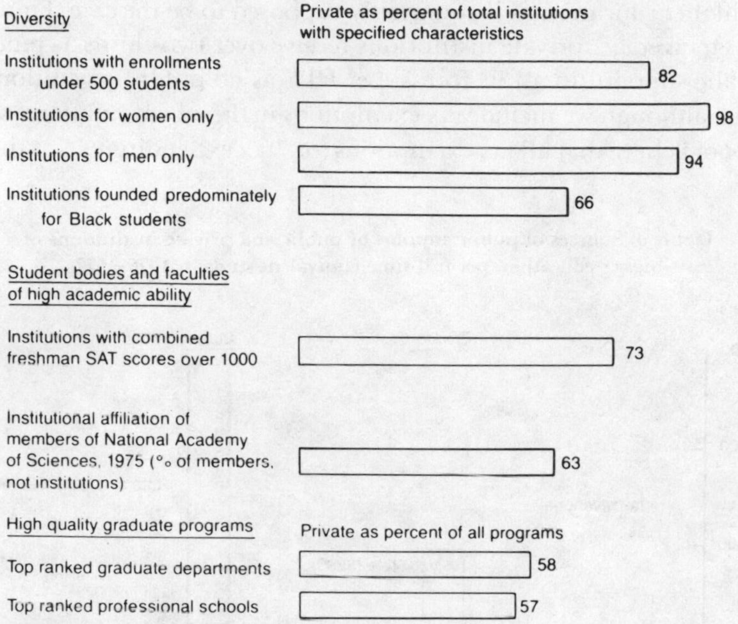

Sources: For men's and women's colleges, black colleges, and small colleges, U.S. National Center for Education Statistics (1975, Tables 97 and 109 and HEGIS data), recent data on SAT scores provided by Alexander Astin; for membership, National Academy of Sciences (n.d.); ranking of graduate departments, Roose and Andersen (1970); and ranking of professional schools, "The Cartter Report" (1977).

The states and the federal government have been quite quickly responsive to the need for financial aid. Public support from all sources (federal, state and local subsidies, and federal, state and local tax exemptions) is not as far apart for public and private institutions of higher education as is commonly supposed to be the case (Figure 3). On average, private institutions receive over two-thirds as much public support, in all its forms, per FTE as do public institutions. And, although we include tax exemptions in these computations, we do not believe that all tax exemptions (or "tax expenditures," as they

Figure 3. Sources of public support of public and private institutions of higher education, per full-time equivalent student, 1976–1977

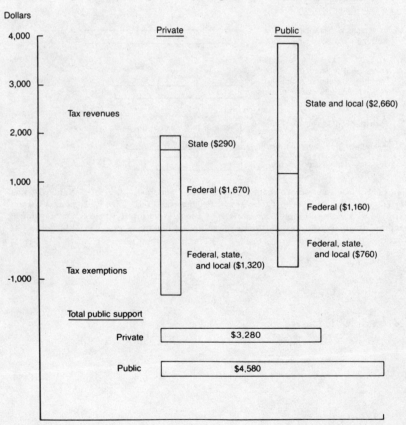

Source: Table 1 (amounts have been rounded to the nearest $10).

are now called in federal budget documents) are equivalent in their impact. Some benefit individuals, whereas others contribute to the general welfare.[3]

The modest reduction of inflationary pressures and the improvement in the level of activity of the general economy have also aided the private (as well as the public) sector—in total, probably more than increased public support has. Yet continued inflation in the future could pose serious difficulties.

As of the academic year 1976-77, private institutions were more numerous than ever before in history, had their highest total enrollments (Figure 4), and in the fall of 1976 experienced a greater enrollment rise than comparable public institutions. Although some institutions have closed (see Technical Supplement A, Table 35) and a significant number of others are noticeably hard-pressed, there is no acute general crisis calling for drastic immediate increases in public support to perpetuate private higher education. There are, however, continuing reasons for substantial concern over the long run.

3. More public assistance will be necessary in the future. In addition to other factors contributing to the prospective economic problems of private institutions, the age cohort of 18- to 21-year-olds, which has traditionally supplied much of the enrollment in private colleges and universities, will decline some 25 percent by about 1995 from its peak level and is then projected to rise gradually (Figure 5).[4] American society, however, will need the enrollment capacity of the private sector when the size of this age cohort again rises after 1995 and when a higher proportion of older adults seeks postsecondary education both before and after 1995. Moreover, it will always need

[3] Exclusion of scholarships from taxation, for example, benefits individual scholarship holders, just as G.I. educational benefits accrue to veteran recipients of those benefits. On the other hand, we find much merit in the argument that tax exemption of gifts to institutions of higher education (or to charitable institutions) does not benefit the individual donors—though they may be induced to give more than they otherwise would have because of the tax exemption—but, rather, contributes to the general welfare by supporting institutions with an important public purpose. Similarly, state and local property tax exemptions contribute to the general welfare for the same reason.

[4] Whether a rise will actually occur depends on the behavior of the birthrate in the next several years. Only very recently have there been indications of a reversal in the downward trend.

Figure 4. Degree-credit enrollment in higher education and number of institutions, by control, decennial, 1929–30 to 1949–50, and annual, 1949–50 to 1976–77

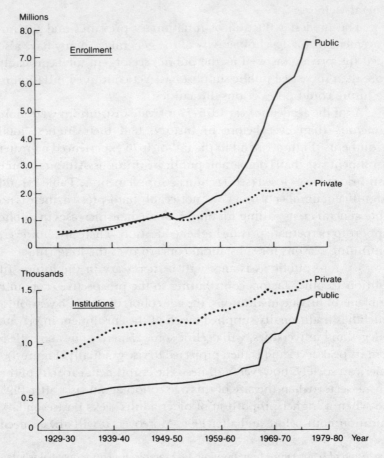

Note: For 1975–76 and 1976–77, degree-credit enrollment has been estimated. From 1974–75 on, branch campuses are included in institution count. Branch campuses were not counted separately in prior years.

Sources: American Council on Education (1973); U.S. Office of Education (1932, 1944, and 1952); U.S. National Center for Education Statistics (1976 and 1977b).

the flexibility the private sector gives to higher education as a whole and the stimulation it gives to the public sector. At all times, American society benefits from the competition between healthy private institutions and healthy public institutions.

Figure 5. Estimates and projections of the civilian population aged 18 to 21, 1950-2000

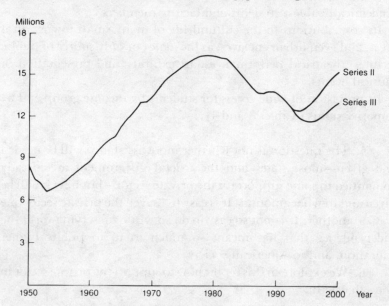

Note: Series II and Series III are alternative projections of future population growth by the U.S. Bureau of the Census; Series II assumes an expected lifetime fertility rate of 2.1, while Series III assumes a rate of 1.7.

Sources: Estimated from data in U.S. Bureau of the Census (1965, 1974a, 1975, and 1976a), and U.S. Department of Defense (1974).

4. We value the private sector for the following reasons:

• Its independence of governance
• Its diversity
• Its long-standing traditions that are so meaningful to its students and its alumni
• Its competition with the public sector
• Its devotion to liberal learning (95 percent of all liberal arts colleges are private)
• Its standards of academic freedom (the American Association of University Professors censured 72 public institutions between 1966 and 1975, but only 28 private institutions)
• Its attention to and attraction for the individual student (Table 2)

• Its contribution of a high proportion of the institutions with the academically ablest students and faculty members
• Its contributions to the cultural life of many small towns, rural areas, and even urban enclaves, as the major or only source of public lectures, theatrical performances, art exhibits, and presentation of musical events.
• Its provision of wide access for students by income group and by minority status (Tables 3 and 4)

5. The question is not whether more assistance will be needed and given—most states and the federal government are already committed to some support for the private sector—but how it will be given and in what amounts. It is easy to "save" the private sector one way or another. It is not so easy to do so while preserving for it the independence that has meant so much to it, to public higher education, and to American society.

6. We explore in this report how to support the private sector in ways that will:

• Be effective
• Preserve its independence
• Encourage balanced competition among private institutions and between them and public institutions
• Avoid "bailing out" individual institutions on the brink of failure, for this will discourage competition

We wish to encourage preservation of those characteristics that make the private sector worth saving—in particular, its independence and striving to do better.

We oppose income tax credits or deductions to offset part of tuition costs because, in their most likely forms, they are clearly regressive—doing more for the rich than for the poor. But we strongly support the continuation of tax exemption of private gifts to institutions.

We favor cooperation, based on a logical division of labor, between the federal and state governments in their policies toward higher education. We believe that the federal government has special responsibilities for (a) support of basic research; (b) support of advanced graduate training and medical education; and, as already suggested, (c) support of equality of opportunity through aid to needy students in meeting their noninstructional costs.[5] The states should continue to be responsible, as they have been traditionally, for (a) basic support of public institutions of higher education; (b) tuition policies in public higher education; (c) planning the development of state systems, drawing private institutions into the planning process and avoiding duplication of their resources and facilities; and, as has been increasingly the case in recent years, (d) aid to needy students in meeting their tuition costs (with federal assistance through the SSIG program).

9. We favor a cautious approach concerning proprietary institutions pending development of means for assuring selection of appropriate programs and for guaranteeing proper use of funds.

10. We note that the programs set forth here are not adequate to meet the special needs of the great private research universities, which must rely more heavily on federal than on state support.

11. We urge that private institutions be fully involved in all state planning and coordinating efforts, and that state systems be planned as a whole. We believe that higher education has entered a new stage of development in which the states should, and will, increasingly look to their total resources for higher education, both public and private, and the most effective joint use of such resources.

12. Any policy aimed at such preservation should observe certain guidelines:

● The first is maximum self-help. Money alone, and especially public money, is not enough. Primary reliance should be placed on vision, ingenuity, and untiring effort. Such virtues are not encouraged by public guarantees of assistance or even survival; they result more from an environment that provides incentives than from one that assures continuity regardless of effort.

● The second is to provide more state support but to move gradually in increasing that support—to ensure the best use of the money by the recipient institutions, to avoid undue disturbance to public institutions and to state budgets, and to reserve some potential for the still

[5] See Carnegie Council (1975c) for more extensive discussion.

greater assistance that will be needed in the years ahead.

● The third is for the federal government to provide adequate student aid, particularly by full implementation of the Basic Education Opportunity Grant (BEOG) program and by very substantial expansion of the State Student Incentive Grant (SSIG) program.

● The fourth is that state programs should be tailored to local conditions and traditions. In Massachusetts for example, a majority

Figure 6. Enrollment in private institutions as a percentage of total enrollment in higher education, by state, 1976

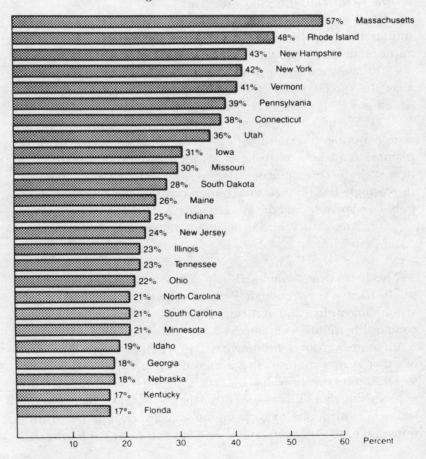

(continued on next page)

of enrollments are in private colleges and universities, while in Wyoming none are (Figure 6). Consequently, no one set of policies can be applied equally to all the states, but certain general directions for action can be indicated. The states are already experimenting with a wide range of programs.

• The fifth is that public policy involves choices of what is best in the long-run public interest and not necessarily what responds to the immediate interest of distressed institutions. Some private institu-

Figure 6 *(continued).*

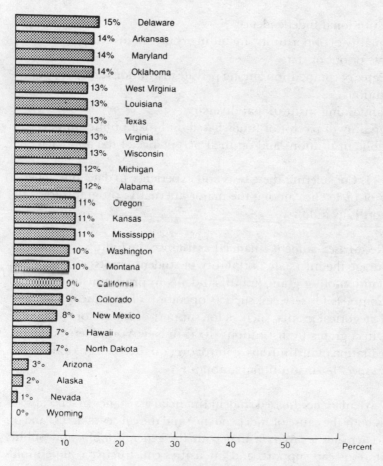

15%	Delaware
14%	Arkansas
14%	Maryland
14%	Oklahoma
13%	West Virginia
13%	Louisiana
13%	Texas
13%	Virginia
13%	Wisconsin
12%	Michigan
12%	Alabama
11%	Oregon
11%	Kansas
11%	Mississippi
10%	Washington
10%	Montana
0%	California
9%	Colorado
8%	New Mexico
7%	Hawaii
7%	North Dakota
3%	Arizona
2%	Alaska
1%	Nevada
0%	Wyoming

Percent

Source: U.S. National Center for Education Statistics (1977c).

tions want money any way they can get it; they feel they are not in a position to be choosers. Public policy requires that careful consideration be given to what is best both for higher education in general and for American society. This is the view we seek to advance in this report.

13. Basic to any choice of one type of state aid over another is the impact the program is likely to have—on the institution, on the student, and on society. Important considerations are the program's impact on:

● Institutional independence
● Equality of opportunity, including choice of institution, whether in-state or out-of-state
● Degree of competition among private institutions and with public institutions
● Maintaining institutional diversity
● Certainty of receipt of funds based on broad public support
● Public institutions and on their acceptance of the approach

14. Considering these tests and experience to date, our general order of preference among the major alternative programs for state support is as follows:

(a) Need-based student financial assistance, including measures to encourage the interstate portability of student grants
(b) Tuition-offset grants for all students in private institutions
(c) Contracts for services, such as operation of a medical school
(d) Categorical grants, such as for support of library operations
(e) Direct grants to institutions (if, as in New York, there is careful accreditation of institutions, control over quality of degrees awarded, and respect for institutional autonomy)

We place need-based student financial assistance first because it helps both the cause of independence and the causes of access and of choice, creates a program that both the general public and public institutions can support, and intensifies constructive competition. We place tuition-offset grants in second place for the same reasons, with two reservations: it may result in less aid for low- and lower-income students, and it places the private and public institutions in a position of potential conflict. We locate contracts for services and categorical grants next in our listing chiefly because they are more likely to assist individual institutions or parts of institutions than the private sector in its entirety. We rank direct grants to institutions last because they move private institutions closer to the category of state-supported institutions (with all the attendant implications for their independence); are not related to student need; and, more than any other approach, are likely to lead to a confrontation between public and private institutions. Moreover, we feel that states should not commit themselves to "bailing out" individual institutions rather than relying on the forces of competition.

A great variety of combinations is possible among the different forms of assistance. We recognize that circumstances in individual states will indicate different combinations of programs and different levels of expenditures in the future as they have in the past. There are 50 different states, and there may well be 50 different state policies.

We call this report *The States and Private Higher Education* because there are 50 states with 50 *diverse* situations. Throughout this report we will note the variety among the states. Recognition of this variety is essential both to an understanding of the problems and to prescriptions for their solutions.

2

The Economic Position
of the Private Sector

The general financial position of the private sector seems to have been most affected by the increasing size and geographical spread of public systems (particularly in those states with substantial private sectors) and by the growing tuition gap; and it is beginning to be affected (as is the public segment) by the slowing rate of growth in the 18-to-21 age cohort and its subsequent certain decline.

The financial difficulties of the private sector of higher education in the late 1960s and early 1970s have been well documented (Jenny and Wynn, 1970; Cheit, 1971; Jellema, 1971 and 1973). After the shock of the first widespread deficits and the dire predictions that followed, many institutions took steps to bring budgets into balance and others exercised caution lest deficits develop. The situation improved and then stabilized by the mid-1970s. The best recent analytical studies are those undertaken by Howard R. Bowen and John Minter (Bowen and Minter, 1975 and 1976; Minter and Bowen, 1977). They concluded that about 25 percent of their stratified sample of 100 private colleges and universities were in serious trouble in 1975. In the two years following, although they found considerable flux among the individual institutions, they concluded that no appreciable change had occurred in the distribution of the sample as among financially weak and strong institutions. As the authors note, they lacked comparable historical data and thus had no basis for judging changes either in the prevalency of distress or in the pattern of flux among institutions.

Enrollment Trends

Enrollments in private higher education have long been a declining proportion of total enrollments; but have increased steadily, albeit comparatively slowly, in absolute terms (see Figure 4). Reversing long-term trends, the comparative size of the private sector rose very slightly in the fall of 1976, since private enrollments increased while enrollments fell in the public sector. (For a discussion of this historical turnabout, see Technical Supplement A.) The most important forces at work have been these:

• Increases in both public and private enrollments have slowed down even though they continued, as the rate of growth of the 18-to-21 age cohort has declined.

• Public enrollments were strongly affected by a sharp reduction in the enrollment of veterans from 1975 to 1976.

• Among the states, private enrollments have tended to rise most where total enrollments have risen most, and vice versa, though there have been some exceptions. In the majority of states, both public and private full-time equivalent enrollments in universities and other four-year institutions increased from 1970 to 1975 (Map 1). Where public enrollments rose and private enrollments decreased, as in Ohio and Indiana, the increase in overall enrollments tended to be slight.

• Among the states, increased enrollment competition from the public sector has had the greatest impact where private enrollments were a relatively high proportion to begin with. This has been especially true in those states in which private institutions draw most of their students from within the state. This trend implies that large private enrollments are more susceptible to public encroachments than are more limited private enrollments; that is, some significant proportion of large private enrollments is vulnerable to competition from expanding public systems.

• State aid to private institutions has not fully shielded them, thus far, viewed state by state and by and large, from loss of enrollments where there has been a fast expanding public sector. In fact, private enrollments generally have gone down as a percentage of total enrollments in states with substantial aid programs. This is related to the prior point; state aid, it appears, is most likely to be given where

Map 1. Changes in full-time equivalent enrollment in public and private universities and four-year colleges, by state, 1970–1975

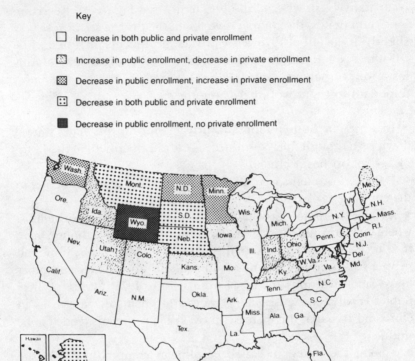

UNITED STATES

Key

☐ Increase in both public and private enrollment

▧ Increase in public enrollment, decrease in private enrollment

▨ Decrease in public enrollment, increase in private enrollment

⬚ Decrease in both public and private enrollment

■ Decrease in public enrollment, no private enrollment

Source: Table 24.

the private sector is large, but a large private sector appears to be particularly subject to erosion of enrollments by an increasingly competitive public sector. The public aid, however, may have prevented still greater erosion. The rule seems to be that a large private sector is vulnerable but also politically influential. The aid induced by its influence has not so far fully offset its vulnerability, but may have done so in part. Let us note quickly, however, that, while state aid may not always have served to increase or even maintain enrollments, it has helped the financial condition of individual institutions.

Technical Supplement A illustrates how misleading it is to overgeneralize about the private sector, for different parts of it behave in quite contrary ways from others—there are more specific exceptions than there are general rules. Some points of special interest are:

● The comparative stability of the more academically elite sector
● The great volatility of behavior of the less selective liberal arts colleges—some going way up and others way down in enrollments, some advancing with new missions and new clientele and some declining
● The favorable behavior of enrollments in institutions responsive to the interests of adult students and the changing interests of vocationally oriented students
● The extreme importance to individual institutions of gaining accreditation status[1]
● The disadvantages of being heavily concentrated on teacher training (like many of the less selective liberal arts colleges)
● The disadvantages of being very small, very rural, or very new; and of being small, female, and Catholic (related, in some instances, to preparing teachers for parochial schools)[2]

Another factor affecting individual institutions is geographical location. It is better for a private institution to be in an area of expanding population—the South or Southwest—than a contracting one. It is better for such institutions to be in an area, other things being equal, where many parents want their children to attend a private college and where public opinion highly favors such colleges, as in the Northeast.

Tuition Gap

Private and public tuitions have, in recent years, generally kept pace with each other in terms of percentage increases; public tuition has

---

[1] Evidently spurred on by the prospect of federal and state student aid, no less than 187 private institutions acquired, through accreditation or preaccreditation status, eligibility for listing by the U. S. National Center for Education Statistics (NCES) between 1970 and 1975. Many of these institutions had been in existence for decades, and some were proprietary (see Technical Supplement A for details).

[2] See Riesman (1975) on these trends.

risen faster, but the private sector started from a much higher base (Figure 7 and Table 5). The dollar gap, as a consequence, has roughly doubled in the past decade. The general burden of all tuition, however, has remained about the same, since tuition costs have risen more or less parallel with the rise in per capita disposable personal income (1970-71 to 1975-76). The total cost of tuition and board and room, however, has risen less rapidly than personal income (Figure 7 and Table 6), and thus the real burden on families and students has gone down, not up, as is often said to be the case. However, as Goldberg and Anderson (1974) have shown, the average family had its children at less than two-year intervals in the 1950s and 1960s and thus may have more than one child in college at one time. For such

Figure 7. Comparative increases of tuition, tuition and board and room, board and room, consumer price index, and per capita disposable personal income, 1970–71 to 1975–76, for four-year colleges other than universities

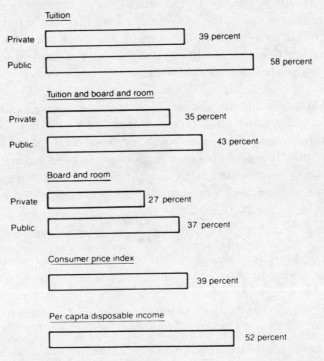

Sources: Tables 5 and 6.

families, the total costs frequently represent a sizable proportion of income.

Individual institutions—especially if their students tend to be state residents—are affected less by the general gap between private and public tuitions than by the gap within their state for comparable types of institution. These gaps, shown in Table 7, vary from $130 to $2,500. Figure 8 shows one of these comparisons, that for comprehensive institutions, which tend to be in close competition for in-state students. Public tuitions tend to be higher in states with large private segments. Thus, it is important to look at the situation state by state as well as overall.

Financial Status

The present study draws on three main types of additional data to indicate the financial condition of the private sector: Higher Education General Information Survey (HEGIS) data on enrollments and finances, including fund balances (available only for 1974-75); survey data from a sample of more than 200 private four-year institutions collected by the Carnegie Council; and site visits to 28 private institutions in states with relatively strong programs of aid to private institutions and to their students.

Enrollment is a major factor in the financial well-being of the private sector. Almost two-thirds of the four-year institutions derive at least 70 percent of their *unrestricted* educational and general revenue from tuition and fees (Table 8). The percentage drawing 70 percent or more of their *total* educational and general revenue from tuition and fees is much smaller—43 percent (Table 9)—but this difference is attributable in part to the relatively important role of revenue received for research in the case of universities and to special factors affecting revenue of certain other types of institutions, as we shall see at a later point. The typical situation is one of substantial dependence on tuition and fees for most private institutions.

In the light of this dependence, the uneven behavior of enrollment in the private sector is a matter of considerable concern. It is true that total FTE enrollment in private universities and four-year colleges increased 3.9 percent from 1970 to 1975 (Table 10). This figure would seem to indicate that the private sector was holding its own. But *undergraduate* FTE enrollment declined slightly, and we

Figure 8. Average difference in tuition and fees: private comprehensive institutions
compared with public comprehensive institutions, arrayed in descending order,
1973–74

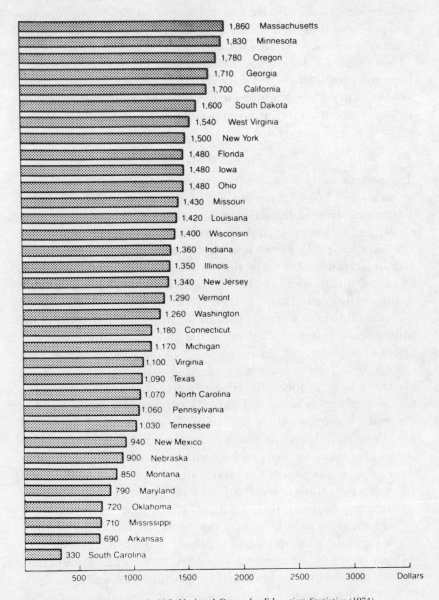

1,860	Massachusetts
1,830	Minnesota
1,780	Oregon
1,710	Georgia
1,700	California
1,600	South Dakota
1,540	West Virginia
1,500	New York
1,480	Florida
1,480	Iowa
1,480	Ohio
1,430	Missouri
1,420	Louisiana
1,400	Wisconsin
1,360	Indiana
1,350	Illinois
1,340	New Jersey
1,290	Vermont
1,260	Washington
1,180	Connecticut
1,170	Michigan
1,100	Virginia
1,090	Texas
1,070	North Carolina
1,060	Pennsylvania
1,030	Tennessee
940	New Mexico
900	Nebraska
850	Montana
790	Maryland
720	Oklahoma
710	Mississippi
690	Arkansas
330	South Carolina

500   1000   1500   2000   2500   3000   Dollars

Source: Computed from data in U.S. National Center for Education Statistics (1974).

have already noted a decline in FTE enrollment in private institutions in a good many states (Map 1). The overall increase masked
what was happening to individual institutions. Both total and
undergraduate enrollments were declining in many private colleges
and universities. Less selective private liberal arts colleges were the
most severely affected; universities, the least. Some institutions
maintained total enrollments by increasing the number of graduate
and professional students, others by enrolling more part-time
students (a volatile enrollment sector). But these kinds of increases
obscure the fact that the bread-and-butter enrollment—full-time
undergraduates—declined even more frequently than total enrollment. (Enrollments have also gone down in some public institutions
since 1970—by 10 percent or more in some 130 institutions, heavily
concentrated among comprehensive universities and colleges).

One would expect that the institutions most dependent on
tuition—the tuition "cluster"[3]—would be the most vulnerable to
public competition. Our findings lend some support to this
generalization. Among four-year institutions, less selective liberal
arts colleges are in the most vulnerable financial position, as well as
in the most precarious enrollment position (for financial data, see
Technical Supplement C). In this respect, our findings are consistent
with those of the Bowen-Minter studies. We found that the
proportion of less selective liberal arts colleges in a weak financial
position is relatively high (29 percent), compared with all respondent
institutions (18 percent). Significant, also, is the fact that most of the
other institutions in a weak position are among the more selective
liberal arts colleges.

As a group, the less selective liberal arts colleges have little
endowment income and, outside of tuition revenue, are heavily
dependent on private gifts, a precarious source of income (Table 11).
Comprehensive universities and colleges also have relatively little
endowment income and are even more dependent on tuition than are
other types of private institutions, but they are somewhat less likely
to be in a weak financial position, probably because many of them
have been successful in maintaining enrollments through broad-

[3] Smith and Henderson (1976).

ening their programs and attracting adult students.[4]

A somewhat unexpected relationship, revealed in Table 9, is that the percentage of less selective liberal arts colleges heavily dependent on tuition (70 percent or more) is substantially smaller than that of more selective liberal arts colleges. Or, to put the matter differently, a surprising fourth of the less selective liberal arts colleges receive less than half of their revenue from tuition.

What are the characteristics of institutions that are not heavily dependent on tuition? Investigation of institutional data reveals that such institutions fall into two distinct groups (with almost no exceptions): small religious institutions (essentially theological seminaries with some liberal arts programs that receive the bulk of their income from private gifts) and black colleges (the colleges founded for Negroes).

Because the financial position of the black colleges has long been a problem of special concern, we also developed data on the sources of educational and general revenue for the private black colleges in 1974–75 (Table 12). Howard University is the only private black institution in the university category and receives the bulk of its revenue from the federal government. Two of the private black institutions are in the comprehensive universities and colleges category; all the others (48 in all) are less selective liberal arts colleges. Only 36 percent of the revenue of these black liberal arts colleges comes from tuition and fees, compared with 60 percent for the less selective liberal arts colleges as a whole. The explanation is twofold: tuition in the black colleges tends to be low in order to hold down the financial burden for the large proportion of their students from low-income families, and the black colleges receive significant support from the federal "developing institutions" program (their revenue from this source appears under "sponsored research and other programs" in Table 12). These colleges are also more heavily dependent on private gifts (24 percent) than the selective liberal arts colleges as a whole (19 percent). The proportion of their students receiving aid is extremely high. A recent survey indicated that more

---

[4] The Council's survey of selected private institutions showed very few comprehensive institutions to be in a weak financial position, although 16 percent were losing ground (Technical Supplement C, Table 50). Minter and Bowen (1977) also show very few in a weak position, but 35 percent to be losing ground.

than nine out of ten students in private black colleges applied for student aid and that over 95 percent of those who applied received some type of assistance (Davis and Kirschner, 1977), compared to 62 percent of students receiving aid in a sample of predominantly white four-year private colleges surveyed in this same study and about 56 percent of undergraduates receiving some type of aid in our survey of selected private institutions (see Technical Supplement C, Table 45).

The rather special position of private black colleges and certain small religious institutions does not appreciably alter the fact that less selective liberal arts colleges tend to be heavily dependent on tuition and also on private gifts.

Our data also suggest that a significant proportion of more selective liberal arts colleges are in a weak financial position (about 17 percent of respondent institutions of this type in our survey). As a group, relatively selective liberal arts colleges receive comparatively more of their income from endowments than do other groups of institutions, but institutional data reveal that they vary markedly in the size of their endowment funds relative to FTE enrollments. Moreover, the higher percentage of their revenue received from endowment income compared with universities is somewhat deceptive because of the very large research component in the income of universities. If we omit revenue received for research (and the closely related recovery of indirect costs) from university revenue, we find that the percentage of revenue received from endowment income by universities is roughly equivalent to the percentage received by selective liberal arts colleges.

Universities also are not in a uniformly sound financial position. Although we found relatively few in our survey of selected private institutions that we classified as weak, our data clearly indicated an enormous variation among universities in the size of their endowments in relation to enrollment. There were also indications, as in other earlier studies (especially Cheit, 1971), that the most vulnerable universities are large urban institutions that have had difficulty maintaining their enrollments in the face of severe competition from low-cost public institutions.

Though not revealed in Table 11, wide variations in sources of educational and general revenue are also found among the four categories of private universities in the Carnegie classification. In

1974–1975, the proportion of revenue received for research varied from 31 percent for research universities I to 5 percent for doctoral-granting universities II. Variations in the percentages of revenue from endowments were much narrower, though appreciable.

Analysis of fund balances can shed additional light on the volatility of the financial position of many private institutions, particularly changes over time. Unfortunately, comprehensive data on fund balances are available for only one year, 1974–1975. These reveal changes in various institutional fund balances from the beginning to the end of the fiscal year. We have developed data analyzing those changes for various groups of private institutions, but we believe that data for a single year may be misleading and have therefore not included tables based on them.[5] Nevertheless, certain comments seem appropriate:

● Half of the private four-year institutions reported a decline in their current fund balances between the beginning and the end of the fiscal year, indicating that they were operating at a loss. Although we do not have complete data for all institutions for any other year, data from our survey of selected private institutions suggest that 1974–75 was a relatively unfavorable year. The proportion of respondent institutions with operating deficits was higher in that year (44 percent) than in every year of the 1970s except the especially difficult 1970–71 (Table 13).
● The change in fiscal condition, measured by the change in the combined current and endowment fund balances from the beginning to the end of the fiscal year, varied greatly among institutional types. Universities added almost $380 per student, on the average, whereas the average for other four-year private institutions was only about $14 per student.
● Institutions also varied enormously within the various categories. Among the universities, for example, the change in fiscal condition ranged from an increase of more than $8,000 per FTE student to a decrease of almost as much. These changes, which may seem

---

[5] Another complication is that not all institutions follow recommended guidelines in handling their accounts and in reporting to NCES, as indicated in American Institute of Certified Public Accountants (1973). Moreover, because of changes in accounting procedures, figures are not always comparable from year to year.

extraordinarily large, tended to involve universities with unusually large endowment funds per FTE. In fact, the enormous variation among both universities and selective liberal arts colleges (the groups with the largest average endowment funds) in the amounts of their endowment funds per FTE is one of the most striking features of the data (Table 14). Moreover, the private universities showed no uniform pattern in the source of changes in combined current and endowment fund balances per FTE from the beginning to the end of the fiscal year; changes were almost equally divided between those reflecting alterations in current fund balances and those indicating changes in endowment fund balances.

One must remember that 1974–75 was an unusual year. Prices increased rapidly, and colleges and universities were particularly hard hit by the rapid escalation in the cost of energy. Moreoever, tradition precludes an increase in price (tuition, room and board) in the middle of the year. It is not surprising, then, that during this sharply inflationary period many institutions carried operating deficits. The great bulk of private institutions have never accumulated substantial endowments or run large current surpluses, and so it is not surprising that in a year of higher inflation they would not accumulate a current surplus or make additions to endowment.

We would expect that signs of economic deterioration might show up not only in financial indices but also in ways that affect the drawing and holding power of institutions, such as the establishment of new programs and the improvement of facilities. When queried about cost cutting, 28 percent of the institutions surveyed did indicate that economies had adversely affected their educational programs, their ability to attract students, or their capacity to retain them, and some checked more than one of these effects. Deferable costs, such as costs for library acquisitions and plant maintenance, can be particularly vulnerable in the shortrun.

But we also found many signs of progress. Institutions improved library structures, added or upgraded computer facilities, enhanced athletic plants, built university centers to boost the quality of life of residents and newly expanding commuter populations, added art centers, and undertook a host of other additions or improvements. In many cases these improvements were viewed as critical to the institution's ability to keep up with competition, both public and private.

Given their present circumstances, what have private institutions done to help themselves, and have they done all they can? Self-help has taken two main forms: efforts to improve revenue and efforts to reduce costs or otherwise use resources more effectively. Information from the Carnegie Council survey and site visits indicates that most private institutions have engaged in both forms of activity.

In the revenue area, private institutions have developed new academic programs and program combinations, and have sought new clienteles. There are many illustrations. In 1974, Mundelein College in Chicago introduced a four-year bachelor's degree program offered only on weekends. Drawing students from downstate Illinois and Wisconsin as well as from the urban Chicago area, the program now has 513 students, of whom 98 percent have full-time jobs and about one-third reside at the college on the weekend. Some commuter institutions, such as Roosevelt University in Chicago, have developed elaborate course schedules for Saturdays and Sundays, in addition to extensive evening offerings. Other colleges have adopted the philosophy that if the students cannot easily come to the college, they will take the college to the students. Hofstra University, for example, has stimulated new interest in continuing education by working with employers and unions and has tailored new programs to serve these new students at their places of work.

Many colleges have developed new programs designed to add to the core of a liberal arts education some instruction in how that education can be applied. In doing so, they have developed a rich variety of programs, such as the internship program developed at Lone Mountain College by Jan Rakoff, that enabled students to receive credit for working off campus in a prospective field of employment. Dickinson College is part of a 22-institution consortium seeking to revitalize and reconfirm the value of liberal learning by raising student awareness of how the skills and knowledge imparted on a liberal education can be used in diverse careers. Hood College has attracted older students by introducing new easy-access programs for those who pass a personal interview.

Almost all institutions at which interviews were conducted, have sought to intensify and improve recruiting activities. Even those that have not yet experienced an enrollment decline are trying to make sure that they do not fall short in reaching their enrollments targets for the next year and that they maintain their contacts and keep their image active. Many institutions are introducing a much greater degree of sophistication into their recruitment activities, adding more staff, developing new literature, making more extensive use of alumni, and reviewing evaluative procedures.

In the cost area, institutions have made modest reductions in staff—less frequently in faculty than in administrative and service personnel. They have also cut support for professional travel, introduced controls for use of the computer, reduced library budgets, deferred increases in operation and maintenance budgets (in some institutions resulting almost in visible shabbiness), eliminated air-conditioning except for computer facilities centers (even in New York City), cut down on heat, reduced expenditures on office services and supplies, and cut student services. Quite commonly, to help maintain personnel flexibility, they are engaging in increasingly rigorous staff planning, utilizing part-time and temporary appointments, encouraging early retirement of staff, attempting to retire obsolete faculty members and tightening up on the bestowal of tenure, introducing new procedures for budgetary review and control, and directing more imagination and effort to fund-raising. But even these policies may not be enough, for as growth ceases, the percentage of faculty on tenure continues to rise in a disquieting manner, undermining the institution's ability to develop new programs and new markets with which to maintain its flow of tuition revenue.

To deal more effectively with their particular problems, some institutions have formed consortia, joining together to maintain and strengthen standards; represent their case to the government, foundations, and other sources of support; share information and expertise; pool resources; and appeal to potential students through comprehensive recruiting literature. For example, the Union of Independent Colleges of Art, a nine-college national consortium founded in 1966, has, among other things, established a common film library and developed a Mutual Application Program. The Christian College Consortium of 38 evangelical protestant colleges was founded to meet the challenge of public higher education, develop a university system of Christian colleges, and carry out generally cooperative academic activities.

It would be remiss to leave the impression, however, that private institutions have done all they can. The ability of colleges and universities to survive as private institutions depends fundamentally on their own flexibility, creativity, good judgment, and determination.

Vulnerability

Our discussion of the economic position of the private sector must include comments about two segments within the private sector—the "less vulnerable" and "vulnerable" institutions. This is a simplistic but necessary division to make. Each institution is unique to some extent, but the institutions in their entirety can be divided into these two broad categories. The less vulnerable category includes institutions with one or more of the following characteristics: high quality, strong religious orientation, long traditions and loyal alumni support, distinctive academic programs, special clienteles, or attractive locations (sea or ski or both, for example). The more vulnerable category includes colleges that have concentrated heavily on teachers' education; some of the urban comprehensive colleges and universities that have little but higher tuition to distinguish them from their public counterparts; and very small liberal arts colleges with restricted programs, often located in rural and depopulating areas.

The states that have shown the greatest vulnerability in the share of the private sector since 1963 (see Technical Supplement A, Table 28) are:

Florida	Missouri
Illinois	New Jersey
Indiana	North Carolina
Iowa	Pennsylvania
Kentucky	South Carolina
Maine	Vermont
Massachusetts	

Those showing the least vulnerability are:

Arizona	New Hampshire
Delaware	North Dakota
Hawaii	South Dakota
Nevada	Utah

We noted earlier that enrollments in private institutions in states with a comparatively large private sector have been more vulnerable to erosion, despite greater state aid to these institutions, than institutions in states with a comparatively small sector. In the latter group of states, the private sector has historically met and survived competition from the comparatively large public sector; consequently, it is generally more distinctive in ways we have listed above and thus less vulnerable. Arizona, Delaware, and Hawaii, for example, are states with small private enrollments and with a substantial growth in total enrollments. North Dakota and South Dakota have small private enrollments and *declining* public enrollments, and Delaware has small private enrollments and only a slight increase in public enrollments. Utah is marked by strong church support for its largest institution of higher education— Brigham Young. The New Hampshire situation is instructive: there has been little aid to private institutions but also little expansion of public institutions, and private enrollments have done better than in some states with much more aid to private institutions but also much more expansion of the public sector.

In the vulnerable states, the public sector usually has developed relatively recently on a large-scale basis and with higher quality institutions. Thus, the private sector is meeting real competition for the first time, and at a time when overall growth no longer reduces the competitive impact.

A state with few or none of the more vulnerable institutions may be able to preserve its private sector through comparatively modest programs of support. A state with many of the more vulnerable institutions faces a much more difficult situation, particularly if, like Massachusetts, it also has a number of less vulnerable institutions. The amount of support necessary to preserve all of the more vulnerable institutions may be much more than enough for the less vulnerable institutions; furthermore, that amount of support—which may approach or be at the level of 100 percent of the support for similar public institutions—may well threaten the independence of the private sector as a whole. In such situations, better alternatives may be: (1) to absorb some of the more vulnerable institutions into the public sector; (2) to let some of them combine with other institutions or even disappear; or (3) to assist certain of them to become more distinctive and thus less vulnerable through support of carefully selected new academic programs or new construction.

In some states, formula aid alone may not be enough; some system of differential and individualized treatment may also be necessary. The private sector, in some situations, cannot be viewed as a unitary phenomenon. Hard choices must be made. Money and money alone, particularly if given on an across-the-board formula basis, may not always be enough.

Outlook

Although we found no evidence that a large number of private institutions are about to disappear from the scene, about one-fourth may be in distress, and many others face an insecure and uncertain future. There are at least seven reasons for this unfavorable outlook:

1. The tuition gap in current dollars between public and private institutions will probably continue to rise, exerting new pressures on students to take their education in public colleges.
2. A big drop in the college-age cohort will come in the early 1980s, making the 1980s, and perhaps the early 1990s, years of greatest trial.
3. Competition based on low tuition costs may become more aggressive as public institutions also feel the impact of declining growth rates.
4. Many institutions have already engaged in extensive cost-cutting, which will diminish their ability to absorb further inflation or loss of enrollment. When an institution no longer has the resources to respond to changing demands, its future is clouded. For many institutions, there may exist a critical level of enrollment loss that would make recovery much more difficult.
5. Reserves in the form of current and endowment fund balances are

low for many institutions, and some are already heavily in debt. However, although financial data can tell us how much of an immediately available cushion an institution can count on, they tell us little about the financial resiliency that underlies the institution's current financial condition or about how quickly and creatively it could, in fact, respond. The cost-cutting that many institutions have already carried out has probably diminished their ability to absorb further cost increases or tuition revenue losses. In many cases, the easiest steps have already been taken.

6. The growth of collective bargaining in higher education may well be a greater threat to the financial stability of private than of public institutions, because the former cannot depend, as can the latter, on increased state appropriations to cover higher faculty salaries and may face increasing resistance to tuition increases. Student consumerism—occasionally manifested in recent years by strikes against tuition increases—may also pose greater difficulties for the private sector.

7. First-generation college attenders may be more likely to attend certain private institutions that are local, or religiously oriented (or otherwise have a "rural" atmosphere), or vocationally concentrated than second- and third-generation attendees, who are likely to look more widely as they make their selections. These institutions, unless they change, are more likely to be "transmission belts" into a pattern of college attendance than permanent beneficiaries of the process of increased attendance on a permanent basis.

Effective self help is the first and the most important assurance of survival and vitality. But self-help alone is almost certainly not going to be enough in the period ahead.

In conclusion, it may be said:

1. The current economic position of the private sector is roughly stabilized.

2. The situations of individual institutions vary enormously.

3. Some vulnerable institutions will lose enrollment or disappear unless they undertake substantial changes in mission or are absorbed into the public sector.

4. The outlook for the next decade or two is one of increasing pressure on resources.

3

State Programs
Now in Place

In 1975–76, 40 state governments combined spent over $500 million on private institutions and their students (Table 15). About 60 percent of this expenditure was used for financial aid to students; somewhat less than 20 percent took the form of comprehensive formula grants for general institutional support (such as "Bundy money" in New York State); and somewhat more than 20 percent was used for specific educational programs, institutions, or purposes. The total expenditures amounted to about $275 per FTE student, compared to about $2,500 per FTE student in public institutions—a ratio of 1 to 9.1.[1] If aid for special programs, chiefly for medical schools, is excluded, total aid per FTE student was about $231.

The states have provided quite different types of support for private institutions and these different types of support can have quite different consequences. The four general forms of assistance are: financial aid to students; general support grants to institutions; support for specific programs or purpose; and indirect assistance.

Programs of financial aid to students[2], in turn, may be classified as:

• Based on need (usually available to students in public institutions also)

[1] These figures are somewhat lower than those in Table 1, which are for 1976–77.

[2] Some states also have work-study and loan programs.

- Based on merit (usually available to students in public institutions also)
- Based on attendance at a private institution (tuition-offset grants)

General support grants may be classified as:

- Across the board to all eligible institutions (on the basis of enrollment or of degrees conferred)
- Selective to named institutions

Support for specific programs and purposes may be divided into:

- Contracts for services, such as operation of a medical school
- Categorical grants, such as for support of library activities
- Awards for construction and renovation of facilities

Indirect assistance includes:

- Tax privileges for the institution, including exemption from property, sales, and excise taxes
- Tax concessions for a second party, such as tax credits or tax deductions to parents or to donors
- Other privileges, such as the right to issue tax-exempt bonds for construction of new facilities, the right to use eminent domain in condemnation proceedings, and the opportunity to make purchases through the state purchasing agency.

Some of this assistance is given according to formula, and some in response to a specific legislative or administrative decision.

Before outlining the essential features of state student-aid and institutional support programs, however, we need to point out that many of the states—especially the larger states—have more than one student-aid program. Some of these programs are very minor in terms of expenditures, providing aid, for example, to orphans whose fathers were veterans. Among the major programs, some are exclusively for students in private institutions, some are exclusively for students in public institutions, and a great many are for students in both types of institutions. Where the programs aid students in both public and private institutions, the relative amounts of aid provided to those in public and those in private institutions are influenced not only by the public-private mix of enrollment but also by the provisions relating to maximum grants. If the maximum allowed is very small—say, $200 to $300—a large proportion of the aid funds is likely to go to students in public institutions, with their comparatively low tuition levels; students in private institutions receive amounts that are very small in relation to their tuition costs. On the other hand, if the maximum is relatively high, students attending private institutions are likely to receive a comparatively large proportion of the aid funds, though not necessarily of the awards.

The effect of these variations is that the relative amounts of student aid going to students in public and private institutions vary enormously from state to state (Table 16). In the states with more than one student-aid program, the distribution of funds depends on the net effects of the combination of programs, some of which may be tilted toward the public sector and some toward the private sector. Four states—Colorado, Hawaii, Montana, and Utah—provided aid only to students in public institutions in 1975-76, usually because of state constitutional barriers to aid to private institutions. On the other hand, South Carolina provided aid only to students in private institutions. Map 2 illustrates the status of state programs in 1975-76.

Under the impetus of the federal State Student Incentive Grant (SSIG) program, which provides matching funds to states for increases in the amounts they spend on student grant or scholarship programs over the amount expended in 1972-73, the number of states providing student aid has increased substantially in recent years, and it was recently suggested that all 50 states would have student-aid programs in 1977-78 (*SSIG Goes Nationwide,* 1977). However, not all of the states provide funds for aid to students in private institutions. In four states—Delaware, Mississippi, Nebraska, and Wyoming—the state's contribution to the SSIG program must come from institutions of higher education rather than from a state appropriation for the purpose. In these cases, the state may or may

Map 2. Programs of state aid to private higher education, 1975–76

UNITED STATES

Key

▨ Institutional and student aid

▩ Student aid only — $150 or more per undergraduate FTE state resident

▨ Student aid only — less than $150 per undergraduate FTE state resident

☐ States with no program

■ States with no private institutions

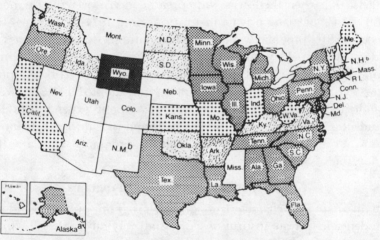

[a] Alaska's program has been suspended, at least temporarily.

[b] New Hampshire and New Mexico added programs for student aid in 1976-77. New Hampshire had a very small program of institutional aid in 1975-76.

Source: Table 15.

not augment a public institution's budget to assist it in providing the matching funds, but clearly a private institution (if it is not the recipient of any state institutional aid) must find the funds on its own as is the case in Delaware, Mississippi, and Nebraska. Wyoming has no private institutions. Because we are concerned with state effort on behalf of private higher education, we have not included matching funds in our table if they must come from institutional sources.[3]

As mentioned earlier, Colorado, Hawaii, Montana, and Utah award aid only to students in public institutions, generally because of provisions in their state constitutions. In addition, Arizona and Nevada had no student aid programs as recently as 1976–77 but evidently have adopted them for 1977–78. Finally, Alaska's tuition-offset program is currently not in effect, as a result of a decision by the state's attorney general declaring it contrary to the state constitution.

The growth of need-based student-aid programs affecting students in private institutions is shown in Figure 9. As we point out in Technical Supplement B, the periods of most rapid growth were 1968-1972, when there was widespread concern over the financial difficulties of many private institutions, and 1974–1976, when the federal SSIG program was clearly stimulating a number of states to adopt student-aid programs in order to receive federal matching funds. The Bundy institutional aid program in New York, adopted in 1968, and the federal SSIG program, adopted in 1972, were landmark developments. Even so, the largest expenditures for student-aid programs continue to be found in California, Illinois, New York, and Pennsylvania, whose programs antedate the adoption of SSIG.

Characteristics of Student-Aid Programs

In discussing the characteristics of state programs providing aid for students in private institutions, we shall rely on Table 17, which gives data for 1976–77 on the largest program aiding students in

[3] In this respect, our practice differs from that of Boyd (1975, 1977), who prepares the annual reports on state student-aid programs, under the auspices of the National Association of State Scholarship and Grant Programs. Boyd's tables show amounts provided by states for incentive grant programs even though those amounts must be provided from institutional budgets, but his reports are oriented more toward amounts of funds available for needy students than state effort.

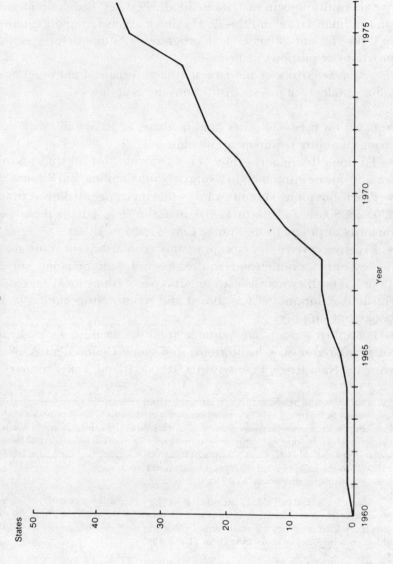

Figure 9. Number of states with need-based programs aiding students in private institutions of higher education, 1960 to 1976

Source: Technical Supplement B, Table 37.

private institutions in each state.[4] In all, 39 states[5] had programs of student financial aid in 1976–77; 11 states had general support grants in 1975–76; and 22 states had programs of support for specific programs or purposes in 1975–76.

Characteristics of the largest student financial aid programs aiding students in private institutions are as follows:

- Based on need—36 states (and of these, 12 have a more or less stringent ability requirement, in addition)
- Tuition-offset grants—three states (provided for all students attending private institutions in Georgia, North Carolina, and Virginia).[6]
- Provisions for maximum awards—maxima range all the way from $200 in South Dakota to $2,700 in California, but in the great majority of programs they range from $1,000 to $1,500.
- Expenses covered—in most programs, scholarships or grants may be used only for tuition and required fees or for tuition alone, but in 13 programs they may be used for all types of educational expenses (including tuition and fees, board and room, transportation, and books and supplies)
- Portability—grants are portable (may be awarded to students attending out-of-state institutions) in 6 states (Connecticut, Massachusetts, New Jersey, Pennsylvania, Rhode Island, and Vermont).[7]

[4] While there would be advantages in relating all of our tables to the same year, our data sources precluded this. Table 15 is based primarily on data for 1975–76 provided in the Carnegie Council's survey of state student financial aid officers and state coordinating councils, which in some cases appear to be more reliable than data based on published sources. On the other hand, it was possible to revise student-aid data to relate to 1976–77 on the basis of Boyd (1977) and Education Commission of the States (1977), and we considered it desirable to do so.

[5] Delaware is omitted in Table 17 because it provides funds only for a small specialized program for orphan children of veterans and a program for students enrolled in out-of-state specialized programs not available in Delaware. Loan programs are not included, although a majority of states have them (Table 19).

[6] Alaska's tuition-offset program is no longer in effect (Table 16, footnote c).

[7] Portability in New Jersey applies only to the County College Assistance Program and to the State Scholarship Program (among New Jersey's major student-aid programs), and in the State Scholarship Program not more than 35 percent of the awards may be used out of state. Limited portability is also possible in a few states—for example, Minnesota and South Dakota—that have agreements for tuition and student-aid reciprocity. Maryland provides student aid to some students coming from other states, but only in two highly specialized programs, one relating to teachers, who must agree to teach in Maryland, and another relating to medical residents, who must agree to practice in Maryland after completing their training.

Table 18 indicates the amounts of student aid in 1975-76 per FTE resident undergraduate in private institutions, and Figure 10 shows the percentages of such undergraduates receiving aid in 1975-76 (Virginia joined the 100 percent category in 1976-77 with its tuition-offset program).

Figure 10. Percentages of full-time equivalent resident undergraduates in private institutions who received state-funded grants and scholarships, by state, in academic year 1975-76

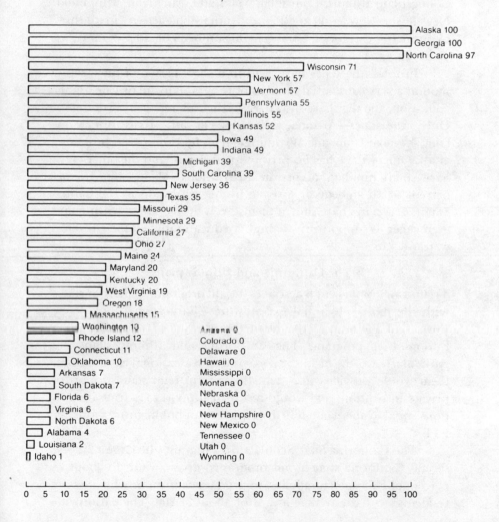

Alaska	100
Georgia	100
North Carolina	97
Wisconsin	71
New York	57
Vermont	57
Pennsylvania	55
Illinois	55
Kansas	52
Iowa	49
Indiana	49
Michigan	39
South Carolina	39
New Jersey	36
Texas	35
Missouri	29
Minnesota	29
California	27
Ohio	27
Maine	24
Maryland	20
Kentucky	20
West Virginia	19
Oregon	18
Massachusetts	15
Washington	13
Rhode Island	12
Connecticut	11
Oklahoma	10
Arkansas	7
South Dakota	7
Florida	6
Virginia	6
North Dakota	6
Alabama	4
Louisiana	2
Idaho	1

Arizona	0
Colorado	0
Delaware	0
Hawaii	0
Mississippi	0
Montana	0
Nebraska	0
Nevada	0
New Hampshire	0
New Mexico	0
Tennessee	0
Utah	0
Wyoming	0

0   5   10   15   20   25   30   35   40   45   50   55   60   65   70   75   80   85   90   95   100

Sources: Carnegie Council; U.S. National Center for Education Statistics (HEGIS) data; Education Commission of the States (1976b).

General support grant categories are divided as follows:

● Across-the-board grants (for all private institutions)—10 states
● Aid for specified institutions only—one state (Alabama)
● Across-the-board *and* aid for specified institutions—two states
(Pennsylvania and New York)

Of the states with some program of support, only nine—
Connecticut, Illinois, Louisiana, Maryland, Michigan, Minnesota,
New Jersey, New York, and Pennsylvania—had activity in all three
of our major categories. For a general summary of aid programs, see
Table 19.

In total, the states have, within a short period of time, set in
motion a very substantial number of programs to aid private higher
education, and they have shown a good deal of ingenuity in doing so.
Only nine states—Arizona, Colorado, Hawaii, Mississippi, Montana, Nevada, Utah, and Wyoming—had, by 1976-77, no programs
at all. One of these has no private institutions, and the other eight
have small numbers of private institutions—62 in all, with 3.4
percent of all students in private higher education in the United
States. The states have shown themselves, by and large, willing and
even eager to support private higher education when the situation
warranted it.

The California and Illinois plans

Technical Supplement B describes the aid programs in the four states
with the most substantial expenditures (California, Illnois, New
York, and Pennsylvania) and in the one state (Georgia) with a
tuition-offset program. The California and Illinois plans are
particularly worthy of study; if extended on a national basis, each of
them would provide more than the current total state support of
private institutions and would result in support of private institutions equal to about one-fourth of the level of public institutions per
FTE.

The California State Scholarship Program (the largest among
several California student aid programs) gives awards to about 25
percent of FTE undergraduates in private institutions who are state
residents, with an average award of about $2,200. The nationwide

cost of a comparable program, if confined to state residents in all states, would be about $520 million for students in private institutions. With all grants portable, the nationwide cost would be about $810 million (assuming the percentage of students receiving awards to be the same for migrating students as for those enrolling in their home states). The latter amount would require an increase of $498 million (over the $312 million expended in 1975–76) in total federal-state expenditures for tuition aid to students in private institutions. In the section that follows, we propose federal matching on a 75 percent basis for all portable grants, as well as a change in the federal provisions to require matching for all increases in state scholarship expenditures from a base date of 1969–70, instead of 1972–73 as provided under existing legislation. On this basis, the federal share of the increased cost would be nearly one-half—even with a base date of 1969–70, the federal share would be held down because there would be no matching for the $190 million spent on state scholarship programs in that year (including all students in both public and private institutions). The increase in the state share would, of course, be divided very unequally among the states. States with expenditures comparable to those in California or Illinois would probably experience little or no increase, whereas states with very limited expenditures per student in private institutions would have to increase appropriations very substantially.

Extending the Illinois plan nationwide would be slightly more costly than the California plan. About 55 percent of FTE undergraduates in private institutions who are state residents receive grants, which average $1,200. A comparable nationwide plan, if confined to students attending institutions in their home states, would cost about $620 million. On a full portability basis, the Illinois plan would cost $970 million if extended to all states.

Impacts of State Programs

It is important to analyze the impact of state programs, but it is also difficult: the programs are new, they are mostly small, and many other forces are at work at the same time. Despite these difficulties, some tentative conclusions may be offered (and are discussed in more detail in Technical Supplement C):

1. State aid is more likely to be given in states with

proportionately large private enrollments, as we have noted earlier, but also in states where private enrollments are more heavily of in-state students. These two points are related. Both encourage legislative interest in the private sector. Enrollments in these states, again as we have noted earlier, tend to be vulnerable to encroachments by expanding public institutions. Consequently, it is not surprising that state aid has not served to preserve enrollment shares in these states, although more losses would have occurred without the aid.

2. Institutional operating accounts over the years do not seem generally to have been substantially affected in states with substantial aid programs as compared with states without such programs. States with heavier aid did incur particularly high proportions of deficits in 1970–71 (another reason why state aid may have been given in these states) but in recent years have not shown an unusual proportion of deficits. This reversal implies that state aid may have assisted these private institutions in escaping the excessive deficit situation. More specifically, the financial situation of many of the less selective liberal arts colleges seems to have been improved by programs of substantial state aid. Perhaps the clearest evidence of this improvement is our analysis of the relative strength or weakness of respondent institutions (Technical Supplement C, Table 50), which shows that the percentage of less selective liberal arts colleges judged to be in a weak position was considerably higher in states that lack substantial aid programs. On the other hand, student-aid accounts run roughly similar deficits in states with and without strong state aid and have increased similarly in both sets of states.

3. Students have clearly been affected by state programs. In states with substantial programs as compared with those without, the percentage of undergraduates receiving grants or scholarships is about 20 percentage points higher; more aid is in the form of grants and less in the form of packages consisting solely of loans or work-study, and more goes to students from higher income families.[8]

---

[8] Private institutions also spend more of their federal student-aid funds on students from higher income families, on the average, than do public: Supplementary Educational Opportunity Grants (SEOG)—$14,000 versus $12,500; College Work-Study program (CWS)/National Direct Student Loans (NDSL)—$17,250 versus $15,250. BEOGs go to students at private institutions with median family incomes of $11,000, versus $9,000 in public institutions; "unduplicated" or mixed account—$12,500 versus $10,250. See Smith and Henderson (1977).

According to available evidence, state aid to date has done more for students (and their families) than for institutions; students have benefited by substituting grants for loans and work-study, and more students from upper-middle-income families have become eligible for aid.

4. The year 1970–71 was very difficult; the next three years were better; the last three years have seen some deterioration again. Inflation levels are the main cause, but changes in enrollment patterns have also contributed. Institutions in states with and without substantial levels of aid have been similarly affected.

5. Freshman applications are down more than are total enrollments. Enrollments have held up due to greater acceptance of transfer students, part-time students, and graduate students. We do not know what impact all this has had on the quality and performance of student bodies.

6. Student-aid deficits of institutions have risen, even with much more federal and state student aid available. Deficits rose by about 50 percent from 1970–71 to 1975–76 in states with and without substantial aid programs. The rise in institutional deficits reflects efforts to offset the impact of rising tuition; the desire to obtain a more diverse student body, including minorities and low-income students; greater competition for the able students; and probably some differential pricing (through student-aid rebates—in effect "buying enrollment") in order to maintain enrollment levels. Federal and state funds for aid to low-income students have released institutional funds for more competitive purposes.

7. The number of institutions in a clearly deteriorating condition is small, but it appears to be somewhat larger, especially among less selective liberal arts colleges, in states that lack substantial programs of aid to private higher education.

8. There are clearly forces at work differentially in institutions of higher education, quite aside from the amount of aid given by individual states.

Tax Exemptions

Any full accounting of public support for higher education needs to examine exemptions as well as public subsidies. Tax exemptions result in revenue losses attributable to provisions of the tax laws that allow a special exclusion, exemption, or deduction from the tax base or that provide a special credit, preferential tax rate, or deferral of a tax liability. Table 20 sets forth estimates of amounts of tax exemptions benefiting public and private institutions in 1976–77. Exemptions amount to about $1,320 per FTE student in private and about $760 in public higher education. The higher rate for the private sector is due mostly to the greater component of private gifts, the somewhat higher family income of students, and the greater value of college property per student. As we pointed out in Section 1, there are important reasons for differentiating among the various types of tax exemptions.

Perceptions of State Programs

The Council's survey of presidential (and financial officer) attitudes toward state programs shows some interesting reactions:

● They have found the programs particularly helpful in increasing revenues for general purposes (75 percent of respondents) and in slowing down the rate of increase in undergraduate tuition (60 percent); in improving their competitive position vis-a-vis public institutions (70 percent); and in recruiting students more successfully (70 percent). Their most general concern for the future is about the prospective level of enrollment (75 percent).

● They are concerned that funding is too inadequate (50 percent) and too uncertain (75 percent).

● There are perceived costs to receiving state aid, in particular: (a) worry over a potential loss of academic autonomy and freedom (15 percent in states with strong programs of support and 5 percent in states with weak programs); (b) increased hostility (10 percent) and decreased friendliness (40 percent) emanating from the public sector; and (c) increased reporting requirements and bureaucratic regulations (25 percent).

● There are changed approaches: more time spent with legislative and other public officials (85 percent); a new use of alumni for contact with public authorities (80 percent); more attention to public relations efforts (60 percent); more emphasis on public service programs (45 percent); and more attention to in-state students— shown by the expectation that an end of state student-aid support would reduce the proportion of in-state residents (95 percent in states with strong programs and 50 percent in states with weak programs).

• Overall, there is no concern that economic developments of the past five years have impaired educational quality (95 percent).

Generally, presidents and financial officers see institutions as being better off as the result of state aid, but also see some danger signals ahead and some clear changes in orientation toward more consciousness of the public sector.

4

Special Concerns About
Public Policy

Many complex aspects of public policies toward private higher
education remain unresolved, and, as we have suggested earlier,
policies vary greatly among the 50 states. Among the considerations
that must be kept in mind in suggesting changes in policies are (1)
equality of opportunity among students from different income
groups, (2) the impact of aid to the private sector on the well-being of
the public sector, and (3) relationships between federal and state
policies.

Impacts on income groups

The several methods of state support of private institutions of higher
education have differential impacts on income groups. For example,
tuition equalization grants apply equally to all students in private
institutions, but a higher proportion of students from the highest
income ranges attend private institutions, and thus families and
individuals in these ranges tend to benefit most. The Council, as its
first choice, and for reasons given earlier, supports need-based grants
to students at both private and public institutions. This approach
will be of greater benefit to lower than to higher income students.
Federal policy has already favored support to lower income students.[1]

[1] An estimated one-half of federal student aid went to students from families with
yearly income below $10,000 and about three-fourths to families with yearly income
under $15,000 in fiscal 1977 (see Congressional Budget Office, 1977, Table 9). Median
family income (1975) was about $11,500 for all families; $13,000 for families with
dependents aged 18 to 24; and $17,000 for families with dependents aged 18 to 24
enrolled in college.

Students from lower income groups go disproportionately to public institutions, sometimes out of necessity rather than choice. It is our judgment that state aid, largely to meet tuition rather than living costs, should parallel federal policy so that lower income students will have a more equal chance not only to attend college but also to choose a private institution if they wish to do so.

While generally favoring emphasis on aid to low-income students, we also advocate gradual liberalization of family income eligibility requirements in the federal College Work-Study program as a means of aiding middle-class students. Moreover, as suggested in Section 3, federal and state student grant funds may indirectly assist middle-income students by releasing private student-aid funds to be used for students from somewhat higher income families than would be permitted to qualify for aid under the public programs.

A number of proposals have been made in the federal Congress and in state legislatures to allow a "tax deduction" for payment of tuition before calculating taxable income or a "tax credit" taken from the amount of tax otherwise owed which would have an even greater impact.[2] Both approaches, and particularly the second, would be regressive in their impacts among families—aiding the rich much more than the poor—and would have negative impacts on public revenues. Even though the tax credit proposals typically have provided for a maximum credit of only several hundred dollars per student per year—a small fraction of tuition in the typical private institution—they would involve costs running several billions of dollars. They also represent an inefficient way of relieving the burden of high tuition in private institutions, because the bulk of the tax credits would benefit the far more numerous families whose children attend public institutions.[3]

Impacts on public institutions

Interviews with public officials did not seem to indicate that state aid to private institutions had as yet (and in the forms thus far utilized)

[2] Unless otherwise limited, the former would permit a person in the 40 percent bracket to save 40 percent of the tuition, and the latter, regardless of bracket, so long as taxes are actually due, 100 percent of the tuition credit actually allowed.

[3] Just as we were ready to go to press, it was reported that both the House and the Senate had included $175 million in spending authority for tuition tax credits for 1977-78, but legislation providing for a program of tax credits had not been enacted, although bills were pending ("Budget Resolutions Cleared", 1977).

negatively affected support for public institutions. Interviews were conducted with state coordinating council officers, staff heads of legislative committees (education and appropriations), and legislators. Interviews were also conducted with representatives of state systems in South Carolina, New York, and Illinois. The first group of people did not believe that the money currently going to private institutions directly or indirectly (student financial aid, direct support grants, categorical grants) had affected the level of appropriations for public institutions. Staff heads of legislative committees pointed out that, with few exceptions, higher education appropriations were not considered as a totality. As the head of one senate committee in New York noted, even when the committee members had a consolidated statement to review, they still did not think in terms of total appropriations for decision-making purposes. In two of three states, representatives of state institutions or state systems did not think that the appropriations to date had injured public institutions. In one state, the view was expressed that anything that the "privates" got came directly out of the pockets of public institutions, although no specific evidence was given to back up this belief.[4]

The main factor seems to be the nature of the legislative process. So far, neither education committees nor appropriations committees appear generally to work in terms of consolidated budgets for all of higher education. Appropriations that go to private institutions either directly or indirectly seem to have no more effect on appropriations for public institutions than do appropriations for other public expenditures, such as for welfare or for parks and recreation. To the extent that all competitive functions impose a claim on state dollars, they all do to some degree affect each other; but the introduction of support for private institutions of higher education appears merely to establish one more claimant for total

[4] Nelson (forthcoming) has undertaken a special analysis of the relationships between funds made available to the public and to the private sectors in states with substantial aid programs and has found in general that the "wage fund" hypothesis does not apply; in other words, there is little evidence that aid to the private sector has been damaging to appropriations for the public sector or vice versa. She does find, however, that New York State is something of an exception, with a significant tradeoff between state support for the two sectors.

state funds rather than to carve off a share of the funds already earmarked for higher education alone.

Nevertheless, there is a danger that support for private institutions could injure public institutions. For this reason, we have cautioned against rapid expansion of state support for private institutions and against forms of support that set the public and private segments against each other.

Whatever the program adopted, fair treatment of the public and private sectors must be assured. For example, it would not be fair if support for private institutions was rising under some automatic formula while that of public institutions was going down as a result of actions, institutional budget by institutional budget, based on the current judgment of public authorities. Such a situation would lead to a quick and brutal confrontation.

There are already ominous signs of the possibility of such confrontations. As was noted earlier, half of the college presidents surveyed in states with relatively strong programs of state support for private institutions report either that hostility is increasing or that friendliness is decreasing in contacts with their counterparts in public institutions.

We oppose raising tuition at public institutions solely to aid the private institutions by closing the tuition gap. We have elsewhere favored low or no tuition for public community colleges (on the grounds of easing access) and a tuition level of about one-third of educational costs (primarily on the grounds of clear private benefits resulting from the education that warrant a private contribution) at public four-year institutions, each on the merits of the situation (Carnegie Council, 1975a, and Carnegie Commission, 1973b). We note again, as we have before, that a number of states have already exceeded these suggested levels, particularly for community colleges.

Portability

About 36 percent of all students in private institutions (and 6 percent in public institutions) attend out-of-state colleges, but there are great variations among states. In 1972, almost 70 percent of all private enrollees in Colorado and over 70 percent in New Hampshire and Vermont came from out of state, but only about 6 percent in Alaska (Table 21). We believe that the opportunity of students to exercise choice outside as well as inside their states of residence is of substantial importance. Such opportunity adds to freedom of choice; is part of the mobility that is so characteristically an American quality; reduces parochialism in points of view; rewards institutions that develop unique personalities and have the highest quality academic endeavors—the best gain the most from portability; responds to interstate division of labor, as in so many other segments of society; and reflects the fact that many colleges are located close to state borders.

This interstate migration, however desirable, nevertheless causes funding problems. It also causes conflicts among institutions. In every state except one (Alaska), private institutions draw more of their students from out-of-state than do public and thus have a greater interest in portability of student financial aid. Among private institutions, moreover, research universities draw more widely than do comprehensive institutions, more selective liberal arts colleges than less selective, and unique institutions than those that are more routine in character. The gain of one institution can be a loss to another.

The national interest lies, however, on the side of portability. It can be accomplished by interstate cooperation—most readily by individual states simply providing reciprocity with other states that also make their aid portable[5]—or by federal action. We believe that some federal action will be necessary and make suggestions below.

Coordination and Planning

From the point of view students, parents, and employers, it is the totality of higher education resources—public and private—of the state that is important; yet, too often, these resources are approached as though they were parts of two separate worlds. They clearly are not. As we have seen earlier, one of the greatest impacts on the private sector, in a number of states, has been the expansion of the public sector. As an illustration, the Chicago Circle campus of the University of Illinois, located within close proximity to Roosevelt and DePaul Universities, began to offer four-year programs in 1961. Between 1963 and 1970, the FTE enrollment at Roosevelt dropped 37

[5] Six states now grant portability (see Table 17).

percent (from 6,812 to 4,282) and at DePaul 34 percent (from 10,272 to 6,688). The fact that Chicago Circle expanded its day programs, which it was originally established to offer, into the early evening hours contributed to this decline in enrollments. There are other illustrations in St. Louis and Cleveland and across the nation.

The public sector, of course, has to expand and must be free to expand. However, some consideration must be given to the impact on private institutions, and particularly when facilities are duplicated, often at far greater public cost. Consequently, we believe that public policy should require advance consideration of the impact of a new location, new program, or expanded program at an old location by a public institution on nearby private institutions (and vice versa) before a final decision is made. One way to ensure such consideration is to make the private segment a participant in all planning processes, as most states now do, although sometimes quite ineffectively (Carnegie Foundation, 1976).

Complementary Federal Programs

Basic Educational Opportunity Grants. After a slow beginning, Congress has moved rapidly in the last several years toward more adequate funding of the BEOG program.[6] Some progress has also been made in liberalizing eligibility requirements. The Council continues to support these and other changes, in line with its earlier recommendations,[7] designed to ensure equality of opportunity for young people from low-income families. We offer two guidelines:

• BEOGs should gradually be restructured to cover the student's noninstructional costs, while student aid designed to help students meet instructional costs should be shifted to other programs, especially the SSIG program.
• For lower division students with full need, BEOG should cover 90 percent of noninstructural costs, and the maximum amount should be increased to the $1,800 provided by the 1976 amendments as soon

[6] Amounts available for the program have increased from $122 million in 1972–73 to nearly $2.2 billion recently approved by the House-Senate conferees for 1977–78 ("Conferees Agree," 1977).

[7] For a detailed account of earlier recommendations, see Carnegie Council (1975c).

as possible. For upper-division students, who can more easily combine study and part-time work, we favor a maximum grant amounting to 75 percent of noninstructional costs. In other words, we favor a "self-help" feature but recommend only a modest self-help requirement in the BEOG program at present, pending more vigorous national policies to improve employment opportunities for youth.

State Student Incentive Grants. The SSIG program should become the major federal program designed to provide freedom of choice among institutions, stimulating the states, as it has already clearly begun to do, to develop adequate student-aid programs. If the program is to fulfill these purposes, certain changes in the federal provisions are needed:

● SSIG grants should be designed to cover tuition and required fees up to a maximum of $1,500, but should not cover any portion of noninstructional costs (after a transitional period during which federal appropriations increase). We favor retention for the present of the $1,500 maximum provided in the present federal legislation, even though it is well below average tuition levels in private institutions (see table 5),[8] because we believe that all students should be expected to rely to some extent on self-help.[9] Moreover, the highest tuition levels tend to be found in institutions that have substantial institutional student-aid funds. As educational costs rise in the future, the maximum should be adjusted upward. There is no reason why states cannot exceed the federal maximum if they are prepared to provide the necessary funds.

● Institutions should not be required to provide funds to match federal allocations (as they are now required to do in a few states).

● Federal matching funds should be available for all increases in

---

[8] This means that the federal matching funds may not finance more than half of $1,500, or $750. If the state wishes to provide for a higher ceiling on a student's maximum award, as some states do, the state's contribution must make up the difference.

[9] Whereas most students are likely to add to their BEOG awards through earnings (especially summer earnings), needy students holding SSIG awards (or both BEOGs and SSIGs) may well turn to loans more frequently to supplement their grants.

state expenditures on eligible scholarship programs from 1969–70 on.

● To encourage interstate movement of students, federal funds should provide 75 percent of the cost of state scholarships or grants for students enrolled in institutions in other states, compared with the present 50 percent matching formula.

● To ensure increased coordination between federal and state student-aid programs, all states should require applicants for state student-aid grants to apply for a BEOG, as 19 states (including the District of Columbia) now do (Boyd, 1977).

● The federal appropriation for SSIG should gradually be increased from the $60 million that has been provided for 1977–78 to about $570 million by 1981–82 (in constant 1977 dollars). We estimate that this amount (along with state matching funds) would meet the requirements of needy students for assistance in covering their tuition costs. The increase would be more than met by savings in the veterans' educational benefit program as Vietnam veterans move into older age groups and exhaust their eligibility for benefits, by a partial shifting of funds from SEOG to SSIG, and by a gradual phasing out of the National Direct Student Loan program.[10]

A few additional comments on these proposals are in order. The Council's earlier recommendation that matching federal funds should be available for all increases in state appropriations for eligible scholarship programs from 1969–1970 on has not, in our judgment, received the attention it deserves. The present provision limiting matching funds to increases in state appropriations from 1972–73 on (or later for states newly entering the SSIG program) is seriously unfair to states like California, Illinois, New York, and Pennsylvania that have had major student-aid programs for a good

[10] For a more detailed discussion of aspects of this estimate, see Carnegie Council (1975c, pp. 33–35). We deduct from our estimate of total federal-state costs an allowance for student aid from private sources of funding, and we deduct from the federal share the $190 million of state scholarship expenditures that would not be eligible for federal matching if the base date for matching were shifted to 1969–70. The estimate applies to costs for all needy students in public and private institutions and thus is not comparable with the estimates of the total federal-state cost of the California and Illinois scholarship plans, discussed in Section 3.

many years and are spending far larger amounts on student aid than most other states. In fact, federal SSIG allocations amount to only a tiny fraction of state student-aid funds in such states, whereas in other states—chiefly those that have only recently adopted student-aid programs—federal allocations amount to 50 percent of the funds (Table 22). Providing for federal matching for increases from 1969-1970 on would increase federal costs by $134 million—the total increase in state funds from 1969-70 to 1972-73.[11]

The issue of portability of grants is particularly complex but extremely important, as already suggested. A federal provision mandating portability (recommended by the Council earlier) seems unlikely of adoption, partly because of its uneven effect on states— states with net in-migration of students would tend to view such a proposal more favorably than states with net out-migration. We therefore believe that a provision creating a strong financial incentive would be more effective. (The higher federal matching formula would apply, of course, to students receiving grants to study outside their states of residence under reciprocity agreements between states.)

Supplementary Educational Opportunity Grants. As the SSIG program is expanded to achieve the objectives discussed above, the SEOG program will be less needed. We therefore recommend the following change:

● Of the funds currently allocated to the SEOG program, $100 million should be shifted to the SSIG program. This shift would more than pay for the additional cost of a more generous federal matching formula for grants to students enrolled away from their home states (only about 13 percent of all undergraduates enroll in other states, compared with about 36 percent of those in private institutions).

Loan Programs. The Carnegie Council has recommended phasing out existing federal student loan programs (the National Direct Student Loan program and the Guaranteed Student Loan program) and replacing them by a National Student Loan Bank (NSLB). We

[11] The year 1969-70 was selected because that is the earliest year for which comprehensive data on state scholarship programs are available.

continue to support that proposal and believe that a combination of two developments will eventually lead to its adoption: (1) continuing inequities, defaults, and other problems in existing student loan programs, which will not be overcome by "patching up" changes; and (2) the continued successful development of the Student Loan Marketing Association (Sallie Mae), which could gradually be transformed into a National Student Loan Bank. However, we believe that the NDSL program should be gradually phased out even before a full-fledged NSLB is established, but not without measures to ensure more equal access to loans by students who frequently experience unequal access—freshmen, very low-income students, and minority students. As Hartman (1977) has pointed out, there are possibilities for modifications in the policies of the Student Loan Marketing Association that would enable it to perform some of the functions we envisage for a NSLB, especially in relation to greater equality of access and alleviation of cyclical disruption in the availability of commercial bank loans. We favor, as part of a policy for phasing out NDSL, the retention by institutions of NDSL funds they have already received as a revolving fund.

The College Work-Study Program. The Carnegie Council has recommended gradually increasing proportions for the College Work-Study program to $700 million and gradually removing family income eligibility conditions (but only as programs for low-income students are more adequately funded), so that this program would provide relatively more assistance to middle-income students. We also believe that colleges should be encouraged to provide compara tively more grant aid to lower-division students and relatively more work-study aid to upper-division students. This recommendation is consistent with our support of maximum BEOGs on a 90 percent of cost basis for lower-division and on a 75 percent of cost basis for upper-division students.

We are pleased to note that the House-Senate conference committee recently agreed on an increase in the CWS appropriation from $390 million in 1976–77 to $435 million in 1977–78 ("Conferees Agree," 1977).

Support of Research Universities. In the area of support of research and graduate education, the federal government has special responsibilities. We have made a number of recommendations, including: (1) that federal funding for research and development activities in colleges and universities should rise along with the Gross National Product; (2) that the federal goverment should adopt a unified program for support of graduate education consisting of merit fellowships, predoctoral fellowships, traineeships, and cost-of education supplements to institutions training doctoral candidates (costing an estimated $180 million); and (3) that the federal government should inaugurate a new program of federal support for research libraries, with an initial appropriation of $10 million.

We are pleased to note that research appropriations have risen at a relatively satisfactory rate in the last several years. We are also particularly pleased to note that the House-Senate conferees recently approved a new allocation of $5 million for research libraries in the 1977–78 budget. In addition, we welcome the new allocation of $3.25 million for fellowships for minorities in the professsions and graduate study that was approved by the conferees—a program that is very much in line with concerns we have expressed for encouraging advanced training of minorities in an earlier report (Carnegie Council, 1975b).

Federal support of graduate fellowships, however, continues to lag, and this had been harmful to research universities. Despite the unfavorable outlook in the job market for Ph.Ds, it will be very necessary to encourage advanced graduate training in order to ensure the development of promising young scholars for tomorrow's research needs.

Because this report is primarily concerned with state policies toward private higher education, we have not devoted particular attention to the needs of private research universities, because their special needs for research support and graduate fellowships must be met in large part by the federal government.

However, expanded funds for state student-aid programs through greatly increased federal SSIG appropriations and matching state appropriations will aid the research universities, though not as much, comparatively, as other private institutions that draw relatively more of their students from low-income families. But our proposal for higher matching funds for students attending college away from their home states will be of special assistance to research universities, which draw their students to a particularly large extent from other states, and also to selective liberal arts colleges for the same reason.

Some private institutions have received special support from their state governments through contracts for special services or through special support for particular educational programs, especially medical education. This type of support can be particularly crucial and has clearly helped to overcome the serious financial problems that some private medical schools were encountering in the early 1970s.[12]

Finally, in connection with federal policies, we wish to express grave concern over the "super-BEOG" proposal that has recently been put forward by some of the associations concerned with higher education. The proposal suggests that the federal government take over primary responsibility for aiding students in private higher education by adding a special tuition allowance on top of the regular BEOG award. We oppose this suggestion for these reasons:

1. The purpose of BEOGs is to assure equality of opportunity in attending college to all young Americans. A clear national promise was made. It would cloud this national purpose to append onto it the "saving" of private colleges and universities. It would obscure the idea of an individual "entitlement" to opportunity by mixing it up with the problem of institutional survival. Administration would be complicated by attempting to serve these two purposes.
2. The politics of support would also be complicated. Public would be set against private institutions and state against state, since many states have few or no private institutions and some have many.
3. Money for access might well be reduced in favor of money for "choice," and access comes first.
4. There are better ways for the federal government to help with "choice," as in the State Student Incentive Grant program.
5. In any event, states determine tuition levels in public institutions, and thus the tuition gap is largely a state problem; the dimensions and nature of the problem depend on the situation in each individual

---

[12] For a more complete discussion of federal and state policies toward medical and dental education, see Carnegie Council (1976).

state. The responsibility for planning the size of the public segment
and the location of individual public insitutions is also a state
problem; and the private institutions basically save state—not federal
—monies in the course of their operations. Only the states have these
three relationships to private institutions. Above and beyond all this,
we have and should continue to have a decentralized system of higher
education and should not move toward a national system.

In conclusion, in relation to federal student-aid provisions, we
stress again the importance of some provison for student self-help,
which may take the form of work-study, part-time work in the private
sector, or loans. Some degree of self-help should be expected of all
students, but upper-division students in particular should be expected to rely more heavily on work-study and loans than lower-
division students.

Federal-state cooperation

We believe, as indicated in Section 1, that some general division of
labor is the best way to ensure reasonable cooperation between the
federal and state governments and to avoid unnecessary confusion
and duplication. Consequently, we support—as has been largely
the situation in the past—the federal government taking primary
responsibility for:

● Support of basic research
● Support of Ph.D. and M.D. programs where scarce skills of
national importance are involved
● Support of equality of opportunity through assurance of necessary funds for student noninstructional costs

We support the states taking primary responsibility for:

● Basic support of institutions as such
● Renovation and construction programs (new construction will
not be an important need in a period of slow growth)
● Financing of community services
● Tuition policies
● Student subsidy, as needed, to meet tuition costs (but with

federal assistance through the SSIG program)
- The planning process

Complex Problems and Complex Solutions

The sources of difficulty for the private sector of higher education are multiple. At the national level, they arise from inflation, recession, the declining rates of growth of the 18-to-21 age cohort, and the recent decline in rates of economic payoff for students. At the state level, they originate in the expansion of the public sector, the increase of the tuition gap in absolute terms, and the decline of total enrollments in some states. At the institutional level, they result in the greater vulnerability of some institutions, particularly the very small, the very rural, the very new, the nonelite, those caught with declining interest in their programs (such as teacher education), those heavily dependent on tuition income, and those with declining religious support.

With several sources of problems, there must be several solutions, and some problems have no solutions. Certainly, not all problems can be solved by state action alone. In particular, not all existing institutions can or should be saved. Each institution makes a contribution to public purposes, but some make a more important contribution than others, and the degree of an institution's importance must be weighed in developing policy.

Broad Alternatives

We have a "nonsystem" of higher education in the United States that is characterized by what might be identified as a "double mix": public and private institutions; and state, federal, and private financial support.

We could elect instead:

1. A "national system," with support only from the federal government. This, however, would reduce local initiative, interest, and competition and would be less reflective of regional variations and differing cultural patterns.
2. A "state only" system, with all public support from the state (and local) governments. Some interests, however, are better handled at the federal level, such as support of basic research, support

of the highest level of academic training, and support of equalization of economic opportunity. A "state only" system would lead to undue parochialism.

3. A "national marketplace" system, with vouchers available to students to be taken anywhere they wished and with no support of institutions as such. This would, in effect, make all institutions private. It would run counter to much of past history, but, more important, would let the market control most or all decisions and thus largely deny public interest in supporting certain services whether or not they draw current consumer demand.

4. A "public only" system, with all private institutions absorbed in to state systems, as has essentially happened in the provinces of Canada. This would clearly reduce the competition between and diversity among institutions.

We judge that the "double mix" system best fits and serves the United States in the current period. We favor movement, however, particularly toward the "national marketplace" approach through (a) greater portability of student grants among states, and (b) a more even-handed approach to competition between the public and private sectors. And, in a limited way, we favor movement toward a "public only" system by having state planning mechanisms look at the totality of higher education—public and private institutions alike. These two directions of movement would allow more effective competition in terms of quality of service in those areas responsive to consumer demand and more integration in those areas subject to public policy.

Need for Moderation

We caution moderation in moving toward each of these two directions. Earlier we suggested particular consideration for the California and Illinois plans for support of private institutions of higher education. These plans would result in state support at a level of about one-quarter of that, per FTE student, in public institutions. If state support were to reach the 50 percent level, we would consider that to be a clear peril point—above that level an institution becomes more state than private in its sources of support. We also note, however, that how the support is given matters a great deal; and we also note that the federal government has come to exercise considerable influence over institutions of higher education at financing levels below 50 percent (and often far below 50 percent).

Finally, we favor coordination of higher education through planning and not through detailed administration (see Carnegie Foundation, 1976b).

5

Recommendations

Recommendation 1. In the broad public interest, the private sector of higher education should be preserved and strengthened in ways that will protect the traditional autonomy of private institutions.

Recommendation 2. Private institutions should utilize self-help to the maximum possible extent and should minimize their dependency on government. To this end, private institutions should continue to seek increased revenues from private sources, improve administration, reduce costs, develop new programs, seek out new clienteles, and plan ahead in order to improve their economic situations.

Recommendation 3. Even with the most conscientious self-help, the long-run position of the private sector is uncertain and insecure. Consequently, more intensive public support of and encouragement for private higher education will be necessary.

Recommendation 4. The federal government should (a) complete the development of its Basic Educational Opportunity Grant program, (b) expand the State Student Incentive Grant program very substantially, and (c) encourage the portability of state grants to students under the SSIG program through a more favorable federal matching formula for students enrolling away from their home states. The BEOG program should become the major vehicle for providing assistance to needy students to meet noninstructional costs, and the SSIG program should help provide for instructional costs. In both programs, there should be an expectation of student self-help—in the BEOG program, through a maximum grant amounting to 90 percent of noninstructional costs for lower-division students and to 75 percent for upper-division students, and, in the SSIG program, through a maximum tuition grant that is below full tuition costs.

Recommendation 5. In the national interest, the federal government has a special responsibility to support research universities—both public and private—through (a) increasing appropriations for research along with increases in the Gross National Product, (b) restoring funds for graduate fellowships to an adequate level (including funding the new program of minority group fellowships), and (c) providing support for research libraries.

Recommendation 6. State governments should act vigorously in developing long-range policies for private higher education, if they have not done so already (in the context of a total plan for higher education), but funding should be increased only gradually as needs become clearly apparent.

Recommendation 7. Financial aid to students should be the primary (though not necessarily the exclusive) vehicle for the channeling of state funds to private institutions.

Recommendation 8. Need-based tuition grants should be the mainstay of state programs of student aid. Such grants should also be provided for students attending public institutions.

Recommendation 9. Need-based state student-aid programs should:

• Provide grants for all students in the lower half of the income range and probably also for some in the lower levels of the upper half of the income range. Grants should be of sufficient magnitude to give students genuine, rather than illusory, choice.
• Provide for instructional and noninstructional costs of students separately (where there is any existing provision for noninstructional costs, as in some of the state programs), pending revision of the federal BEOG program to provide adequately for noninstructional

costs. After that, state grants should cover only instructional costs.
● Provide for a maximum tuition grant of approximately $1,500, the present maximum under the federal SSIG program, although some states may wish to set a somewhat higher maximum. But state policies should allow for significant self-help from students in the form of part-time work or borrowing. Moreover, private institutions with above-average tuition charges tend to have institutional student-aid funds that are used to supplement student aid from public funds. As tuition levels rise in the future, the $1,500 maximum should be adjusted upward.

Recommendation 10. As supplemental forms of aid, to be included where appropriate in a rounded package, the Council recommends:

● Contracts with private institutions for educational and other services
● Categorical grants for selected programs, such as library activities
● Awards for construction, renovation, and purchases of major equipment

Recommendation 11. The Council urges the states to provide funds in modest amounts, to both public and private institutions, to encourage innovation and experimentation in academic programs. Such funds would augment those provided by the federal Fund for Improvement of Postsecondary Education (FIPSE).

Recommendation 12. Grants for direct institutional support should be provided only where there are adequate protections for autonomy and quality.

Recommendation 13. State policies should contemplate special measures, as necessary, (1) to make it possible for selected private institutions to shift to public support (where their contributions as private institutions are not unique); (2) to assist private institutions with weak financial prospects or inadequate academic programs (or both) to merge with other institutions or to phase out their operations in an orderly fashion;[1] and (3) to strengthen marginal

[1] For a discussion of this range of problems, see New York State (1975).

institutions whose continued existence is deemed important through temporary support of planned programs for expansion, revision of academic programs, or improvement of physical facilities. State policies should not, however, contemplate "bailing out" all weak private institutions.

Recommendation 14. State aid to private institutions should not reach such levels and take such forms that they become more public than private in their operations. We suggest that a state subsidy amounting to about 50 percent of the educational subsidy per student in a comparable public institution may be a reasonable maximum.

Recommendation 15. Aid to private institutions should not be given in such ways and in such amounts as to cause significant disadvantage to public institutions.

Recommendation 16. Tuition levels in public institutions should be set on their own merits and not specifically to aid private institutions.

Recommendation 17. The Council is opposed to either tax credits or tax deductions to offset tuition costs, but we strongly support the continuation of tax exemption of private gifts to institutions of higher education.

Recommendation 18. To the maximum possible extent, state programs of student aid should be neutral in their effects on the interstate flow of students. That is, they should neither encourage nor discourage interstate mobility. In addition to proposing a more favorable federal formula for portable grants under SSIG, the Council recommends that the Education Commission of the States encourage interstate agreements for student financial aid reciprocity. Residents of one state choosing to attend institutions in another state should be eligible for financial aid from their own state if the receiving state also provides for grant portability. The Council recognizes that some states are characterized by net out-migration of students, while others experience net in-migration—a consideration that strengthens the case for a special federal incentive for portability through SSIG.

Recommendation 19. Private colleges and universities should be exempt from property, sales, and other state and local taxes on the same basis as public institutions. If public institutions do not have to pay certain taxes, neither, under similar circumstances, should private institutions. (Where payments in lieu of taxes are made for special services such as fire protection, public and private institutions should be treated alike.)

Recommendation 20. Coordinating councils, governors, and legislatures should insist that in decisions relating to the expansion of public institutions or their programs, the effects on private institutions should be taken into account. Similarly, private institutions should consult with their public counterparts on plans for program change.

Recommendation 21. Private colleges and universities should be fully represented in all state coordinating mechanisms.

Glossary

Federal Programs for Student Assistance

BEOG: Basic Educational Opportunity Grants, first authorized in the Educational Amendments of 1972 and since extended, entitle each student in attendance at an institution of higher education to a basic grant, initially calculated by deducting the amount the family of that student can reasonably be expected to contribute toward his education from a statutory maximum, the amount of the grant not to exceed one-half the actual cost of attendance. The 1976 Education Amendments authorized a maximum grant of $1,800, which has not been fully funded. Approximately two million students are eligible for grants.

SEOG: Supplemental Educational Opportunity Grants are designed (1) to supplement the basic grants received by students, and (2) to assist students who are in attendance at institutions of higher education and who do not receive basic grants but are in need of financial assistance. Maximum award is $1,500.

SSIG: State Student Incentive Grants, included in the federal aid package in 1972, provide matching grants to states on a formula basis "to assist them in providing grants to eligible students in attendance at institutions of higher education." Recipients, selected on the basis of need, must be undergraduate students.

CWS: College Work-Study funds allow needy students to supplement other resources by working at part-time jobs in educational and other public or nonprofit institutions. Federal funds supply 80 percent of wages, with the remainder coming from employers.

GSL: Guaranteed Student Loan programs provide federally insured, reinsured, and interest-subsidized loans to students. Programs are either conducted directly by the Office of Education or by state agencies. The aggregate amount of insured loans may not exceed $7,500 to undergraduates and $15,000 to graduate and professional students.

NDSL: The National Direct Student Loan Program is designed to stimulate and assist in the establishment and maintenance of funds at college and universities to provide low-interest loans to students.

NSLB: The National Student Loan Bank, recommended by the Council and also recommended earlier by the Carnegie Commission, would be a nonprofit, private corporation established by the federal government and financed by the sale of governmentally guaranteed securities. Borrowers would be required to make repayments in proportion to their income but in every case would be liable for the repayment of the entire loan and accrued interest. Thus, those with low incomes would require a longer average repayment period than those with high incomes. The average period of repayment would be about 20 years. There would be no interest subsidy and no needs test, but interest obligations could be deferred until after the student's graduation. Repayments would be through the Internal Revenue Service.[1]

Other Abbreviations Used

FTE: Full-time equivalent, used in enrollment, faculty, and financial data to convert part-time participation to its full-time equivalent.

HEGIS: Higher Education General Information Survey, an annual assessment of higher education in the United States conducted by NCES. Data are collected and published on enroll-

---

[1] See Carnegie Council (1975c) for further details.

ments, faculty, finances, physical facilities, library resources, and the like.

NCES: National Center for Education Statistics, an educational
data collection and dissemination agency in the U.S.
Department of Health, Education and Welfare.

Statistical Tables

**Table 1. Sources of public support of public and private institutions
of higher education, 1976-77**

Source of support	Total amounts (in millions)		Amounts per FTE^a		Private as percent of public per FTE
	Public	Private	Public	Private	
Tax revenues	$23,987	$3,805	$3,820	$1,960	51%
State and local funds[b]	16,698	567	2,660	290	11
Institutional support	16,400	220	2,610	110	4
Student aid[c]	298	347	50	180	360
Federal funds[d]	7,289	3,238	1,160	1,670	144
Institutional support (excluding research and student aid)	2,045	904	325	470	145
Indirect student aid	625	326	100	170	170
Direct student aid	4,619	2,008	735	1,030	140
Tax exemptions	4,794	2,565	764	1,322	173
Federal, direct	1,080	1,280	172	660	384
Federal, indirect	1,435	45	229	23	10
State and local	2,279	1,240	363	639	176
Grand total	28,781	6,370	4,584	3,282	72

[a] FTE = full-time equivalent enrollment.

[b] Local funds to private institutions (primarily contracts for services) are not included.

[c] Federal allocations to the State Student Incentive Grant program are included in state funds, as in the annual reports on state scholarship programs issued by J. D. Boyd of the Illinois State Scholarship Commission. State student-aid funds include awards made directly to students and student-aid funds allocated to institutions.

[d] If research is included, total federal funds are $9.3 billion for public institutions and $4.7 billion for private institutions; on a per FTE basis, the amounts are $1,480 for public institutions and $2,420 for private institutions. These additions bring total public support of private institutions to $4,030 per FTE, or 82 percent of the total of $4,900 per FTE provided for public institutions. Federal funds have been allocated between public and private institutions on the basis of data presented in Nelson (forthcoming).

Sources: Carnegie Council survey (1975-76 data provided in Council's survey have been adjusted to probable 1976-77 amounts); Boyd (1977); U.S. National Center for Education Statistics (1977a and 1977d); *Special Analyses: Budget of the United States Government* (1977); Sunley (forthcoming); Nelson (forthcoming); and "U.S. Funds for Higher Education" (1977).

Table 2. Student satisfaction in public and private four-year institutions, 1975

Undergraduate responses to Carnegie Council survey of students and faculty	PUBLIC			PRIVATE		
	Research and doctoral-granting universities	Comprehensive colleges and universities	Liberal arts colleges	Research and doctoral-granting universities	Comprehensive colleges and universities	Liberal arts colleges
Satisfied with "overall evaluation of your college"	70%	67%	63%	74%	74%	75%
Satisfied with "teaching"	63	66	73	76	65	80
Students not treated "like numbers in a book"	36	53	62	57	73	88
Satisfied with "methods of grading and evaluation"	34	52	63	57	59	63

Source: Carnegie Council survey.

Table 3. Percentage distribution of full-time freshmen by size of
family income and type of institution, 1975

	Four-year colleges				Universities	
	Public	*Private*			*Public*	*Private*
Family income		*Protestant*	*Catholic*	*Nonsectarian*		
Under $10,000	23	20	18	16	13	12
$10,000 to $19,999	40	40	40	36	38	30
$20,000 or more	37	40	42	48	49	58

Source: Astin, King, and Richardson (1975).

Table 4. Minority enrollment as percentage of total full-time
enrollments in institutions of higher education, 1972 and 1974

Year	*Public institutions*	*Private institutions*
1972	10.5	12.4
1974	13.6	12.9

Note: Minorities include blacks, Spanish-surnamed Americans, Asian
Americans, and American Indians.

Source: U.S. Office for Civil Rights (1976, Tables 10 and 11).

Table 5. Tuition and required fees in universities and other four-year colleges, by control, consumer price index, and per capita disposable income, 1965-66 to 1975-76 (in current dollars)

Type of institution and year	Tuition and required fees				Percentage increase		Percentage increase[a]	
	Public	Private	Ratio private to public	Dollar gap	Public	Private	CPI	PCI
Universities								
1965-66	$327	$1,369	4.2	$1,042				
1970-71	478	1,980	4.1	1,502	46	45	24	38
1975-76	656	2,775	4.2	2,119	37	40	39	52
Other four-year colleges								
1965-66	240	1,086	4.5	846				
1970-71	332	1,603	4.8	1,271	38	48	24	38
1975-76	526	2,233	4.2	1,707	58	39	39	52

[a] CPI = Consumer Price Index, U.S. Bureau of Labor Statistics; PCI = per capita disposable personal income, U.S. Bureau of Economic Analysis (Department of Commerce).

Sources: U.S. National Center for Education Statistics (1977d, Table 41); the President (1977).

Table 6. Tuition and required fees and board and room in universities and other four-year colleges, by control, consumer price index, and per capita disposable income, 1965-66 to 1975-76 (in current dollars)

Type of institution and year	Tuition, board and room				Percentage increase		Percentage increase[a]	
	Public	Private	Ratio private to public	Dollar gap	Public	Private	CPI	PCI
Universities								
1965-66	$1,105	$2,316	2.1	$1,211				
1970-71	1,478	3,159	2.1	1,681	34	36	24	38
1975-76	1,993	4,298	2.2	2,355	31	36	39	52
Other four-year colleges								
1965-66	902	1,897	2.1	995				
1970-71	1,208	2,599	2.2	1,391	34	37	24	38
1975-76	1,722	3,499	2.0	1,777	43	35	39	52

a CPI = Consumer Price Index, U.S. Bureau of Labor Statistics; PCI = per capita disposable personal income, U.S. Bureau of Economic Analysis.

Sources: U.S. National Center for Education Statistics (1977d, Table 41); the President (1977).

Table 7. Average tuition-and-fee differentials between private and public
institutions, by state and institutional category, 1973-74
(arrayed in descending order of university differential)

State	Between private universities and highly selective liberal arts colleges and public universities	Between private and public comprehensive institutions	Between private selective liberal arts colleges and public comprehensive institutions
Rhode Island	$2,490		$1,340
Vermont	2,460	$1,290	1,270
New Hampshire	2,310		1,490
Massachusetts	2,240	1,860	1,620
Colorado	2,220		1,340
Connecticut	2,220	1,180	1,290
Maine	2,200		1,800
Louisiana	2,180	1,420	900
Florida	2,150	1,480	990
Virginia	2,090	1,100	850
California	2,060	1,700	1,660
Oregon	2,020	1,780	990
North Carolina	2,010	1,070	1,060
Iowa	1,940	1,480	1,100
Tennessee	1,930	1,030	920
Wisconsin	1,890	1,400	970
Ohio	1,860	1,480	1,190
New Jersey	1,840	1,340	950
Georgia	1,820	1,710	1,050
Indiana	1,820	1,360	880
Illinois	1,790	1,350	1,220
Missouri	1,750	1,430	1,220
Maryland	1,680	790	1,000
New York	1,660	1,500	1,180
Minnesota	1,610	1,830	1,130

Table 7. *(continued)*

State	Between private universities and highly selective liberal arts colleges and public universities	Between private and public comprehensive institutions	Between private selective liberal arts colleges and public comprehensive institutions
Texas	1,610	1,090	990
Pennsylvania	1,540	1,060	1,070
Washington	1,520	1,260	830
Kentucky	1,430		960
Michigan	1,290	1,170	1,180
South Carolina	1,260	330	900
Oklahoma	750	720	580
Utah	130		900
South Dakota		1,600	1,020
West Virginia		1,540	1,490
New Mexico		940	450
Nebraska		900	1,020
Montana		850	1,060
Mississippi		710	800
Arkansas		690	570
Delaware			1,560
Arizona			1,500
Idaho			1,490
District of Columbia			1,410
Hawaii			970
Kansas			950
North Dakota			780
Alabama			690
Nevada			670

Source: Computed from data in U.S. National Center for Education Statistics.

The States and Private Higher Education

Table 8. Percentage of unrestricted educational and general revenue
of private universities and four-year colleges received from tuition
and required fees, by type of institution, 1974-75

Percentage of revenue	Total	Universities[a]	Comprehensive universities and colleges[a]	Liberal Arts Colleges I[a]	Liberal Arts Colleges II[a]
Total					
Number	908	60	144	138	566
Percent	100.0	100.0	100.0	100.0	100.0
0.0 to 29.9	3.9	5.0	0.7	0.7	5.3
30.0 to 49.9	7.2	10.0	2.8	3.6	8.9
50.0 to 59.9	8.0	18.3	2.8	8.0	8.3
60.0 to 69.9	16.7	20.0	6.3	15.2	19.4
70.0 to 79.9	22.4	20.0	12.5	26.8	24.0
80.0 to 89.9	27.3	21.7	44.4	34.9	21.7
90.0 to 99.9	13.2	5.0	29.8	9.4	10.8
100.0	1.3	0.0	0.7	1.4	1.6
70.0 or more	64.2	46.7	87.4	72.5	58.1

[a] The Carnegie Commission on Higher Education (1973a) classified (1) four groups of universities, all of which are doctoral-granting institutions; (2) comprehensive universities and colleges, which offer a liberal arts program as well as one or more professional programs; (3) Liberal Arts Colleges I, which rank high on a national index of student selectivity or are among 200 leading baccalaureate-granting institutions in terms of numbers of their graduates receiving Ph.D.s at leading universities; (4) Liberal Arts Colleges II—all liberal arts colleges not meeting the criteria for inclusion in the first group; (5) two-year institutions; and (6) specialized institutions—specialized professional institutions that do not have a liberal arts program.

Source: Adapted from U.S. National Center for Education Statistics (HEGIS) data.

Table 9. Percentage of total educational and general revenue of private universities
and four-year colleges received from tuition and required fees,
by type of institution, 1974-75

Percentage of revenue	Total	Universities[a]	Comprehensive universities and colleges[a]	Liberal Arts Colleges I[a]	Liberal Arts Colleges II[a]
Total					
Number	908	60	144	138	566
Percent	100.0	100.0	100.0	100.0	100.0
0.0 to 29.9	6.9	28.2	1.4	0.7	7.6
30.0 to 49.9	14.7	26.7	6.3	8.6	17.0
50.0 to 59.9	14.0	16.7	7.6	18.1	14.3
60.0 to 69.9	21.4	11.7	15.3	23.9	23.3
70.0 to 79.9	22.8	10.0	24.3	32.8	21.5
80.0 to 89.9	16.1	6.7	37.4	14.5	12.0
90.0 to 99.9	3.2	0.0	7.0	0.7	3.2
100.0	0.9	0.0	0.7	0.7	1.1
70.0 or more	43.0	16.7	69.4	48.7	37.8

[a] See note to Table 8.

Source: Adapted from U.S. National Center for Education Statistics (HEGIS) data.

Table 10. Percentage of states in which private universities and four-year colleges
experienced a decline in aggregate full-time-equivalent enrollment, 1970 to 1975,
by type of institution and level of enrollment

	Number of states with specified type of private institution	Percent of states with decline	
		Undergraduate FTE enrollment	Total FTE enrollment
Universities	24	38	29
Comprehensive institutions	36	67	31
Highly selective liberal arts colleges	28	36	32
Other liberal arts colleges	49	49	37
Senior institutions combined	49	47	35
Aggregate change in FTE enrollment, all states combined		−0.6%	+3.9%

Source: Adapted from U.S. National Center for Education Statistics (HEGIS) data (data exclude the District of Columbia).

Table 11. Sources of educational and general revenue of private institutions of higher education, by type, 1974-75

Source	Total	Universities[a]	Comprehensive universities and colleges[a]	Liberal Arts Colleges I[a]	Liberal Arts Colleges II[a]	Two-year institutions[a]	Specialized institutions[a]
Total							
Amount (in millions)	$8,411.7	$3,937.8	$1,245.3	$758.2	$1,315.7	$224.5	$930.2
Percent	100.0	100.0	100.0	100.0	100.0	100.0	100.0
Tuition and fees	48.4	35.8	69.9	62.7	60.5	65.0	40.5
Government appropriations	3.5	3.4	3.2	1.1	3.5	3.7	5.7
Federal	1.6	1.7	0.8	0.2	2.9	1.2	1.4
State	1.9	1.7	2.4	0.9	0.6	1.7	4.3
Local	_b	_b	_b	0.0	_b	0.8	_b
Endowment income	7.2	9.0	3.9	12.9	3.6	2.4	5.9
Private gifts and contracts	14.1	13.1	8.9	14.1	18.6	15.0	18.5
Sponsored research and other programs	17.0	25.8	7.4	4.1	8.6	8.4	17.3
Recovery of indirect costs	3.5	5.7	1.0	0.5	0.7	0.9	3.3
Sales and services of educational departments	2.2	3.4	1.3	0.6	0.7	0.7	1.7
Other	4.3	3.8	4.4	4.0	3.8	3.9	7.1

[a] See note to Table 8.
[b] Less than 0.05 percent.

Source: Adapted from U.S. National Center for Education Statistics (HEGIS) data.

Table 12. Sources of educational and general revenue of private black senior
institutions of higher education, by type, 1974-75

Source	Total	Universities[a]	Comprehensive Universities and Colleges[a]	Liberal Arts Colleges II[a]
Total				
Amount (in millions)	$271.4	$81.3	$25.7	$164.4
Percent	100.0	100.0	100.0	100.0
Tuition and fees	29.6	14.3	33.5	36.4
Governmental appropriations	21.2	60.2	4.3	4.5
Federal	19.8	60.2	0	2.9
State	1.3	0	4.3	1.5
Local	0.1	0	0	0.1
Endowment income	2.8	0.2	9.2	3.1
Private gifts and contracts	16.7	3.8	12.8	23.7
Sponsored research and other programs	26.0	19.7	29.6	28.5
Recovery of indirect costs	1.4	1.1	6.5	0.9
Sales and services of educational departments	0.5	0.3	2.9	0.3
Other	1.8	0.4	1.2	2.6

[a] See note to Table 8.

Source: Adapted from U.S. National Center for Education Statistics (HEGIS) data.

Table 13. Percentage of respondent institutions reporting operating
surpluses or deficits, 1970-71 to 1976-77
(number of respondents = 151)

		Percent		
Year	Total	Surplus	Zero Balance	Deficit
1970-71	100	46	3	51
1971-72	100	58	4	38
1972-73	100	62	4	34
1973-74	100	58	4	38
1974-75	100	51	5	44
1975-76	100	54	12	34
1976-77	100	51	21	28

Source: Carnegie Council survey. Institutions' reports of surpluses or deficits for 1975-76 and
1976-77 were in some cases based on estimates.

Table 14. Percentage distribution of endowment funds per full-time-equivalent
student, private universities and selective liberal arts colleges, 1974-75
(end of year balance)

Amount	Universities	Selective Liberal Arts Colleges
Total		
Number	61	133
Percent	100.0	100.0
$40,000 or more	8.2	4.5
30,000 to 39,999	6.6	2.3
20,000 to 29,999	9.8	9.0
10,000 to 19,999	14.8	18.0
5,000 to 9,999	11.5	22.6
1,000 to 4,999	37.6	27.8
0 to 999	11.5	15.8

Source: Adapted from U.S. National Center for Education Statistics (HEGIS) data.

Table 15. State aid for private institutions, by state and type of payment, 1975-76 (in thousands of dollars)

State	Student financial aid	General institutional aid		Grants for specific programs or purposes	Total amount	Aid per FTE[a]		
		All private institutions	Selected private institutions			Student	Institutional	Total
United States (50 states)	$311,927	$95,820	$36,526	$69,696	$513,969	$ 168	$108	$ 276
Alabama	70	—	2,003	40	2,113	4	117	121
Alaska	1,300[b]	—	—	237	1,537	1,484	270	1,754
Arizona	—	—	—	—	—	—	—	—
Arkansas	118	—	—	—	118	13	—	13
California	42,030	—	—	1,500[c]	42,030	314	11	325
Colorado	3,868	572	—	94	4,534	94	16	110
Connecticut								
Delaware	9	—	—	—	9	3	—	3
Florida	1,634	—	—	4,144	5,778	34	85	119
Georgia	5,756	—	—	520	6,276	206	19	225
Hawaii	—	—	—	—	—	—	—	—
Idaho	20	—	—	—	20	3	—	3
Illinois	40,800	6,768	—	11,000	58,568	366	59	425
Indiana	8,291	—	—	—	8,291	178	—	178
Iowa	9,269	—	—	750	10,019	274	23	307
Kansas	3,005	—	—	—	3,005	253	—	253
Kentucky	849	—	—	—	849	50	—	50
Louisiana	64	1,600	—	625	2,289	4	126	130
Maine	382	—	—	—	382	43	—	43
Maryland	1,154	4,400	—	—	5,554	55	209	264
Massachusetts	9,410	—	—	—	9,410	56	—	56
Michigan	13,627	1,970	—	842	16,439	269	56	325
Minnesota	5,754	3,210	—	1,200	10,164	172	132	304
Mississippi	—	—	—	—	—	—	—	—
Missouri	2,852	—	—	—	2,852	55	—	55
Montana	—	—	—	—	—	—	—	—
Nebraska	—	—	—	—	—	—	—	—

State							
Nevada	—	—	—	—	—	—	—
New Hampshire[d]	—	—	—	50	50	—	3
New Jersey	8,961	6,000	—	1,221	16,182	177	143
New Mexico[d]	—	—	—	—	—	—	—
New York	73,950	57,400	500	14,500	146,350	248	243
North Carolina	8,789	—	—	2,163	10,952	183	45
North Dakota	20	—	—	—	20	11	—
Ohio	8,396	—	—	6,596	14,992	100	84
Oklahoma	207	—	—	—	207	12	12
Oregon	567	1,900	—	—	2,467	41	137
Pennsylvania	33,853	12,000	34,023	3,200	83,076	226	329
Rhode Island	1,000	—	—	715	1,715	36	26
South Carolina	7,382	—	—	88	7,470	320	4
South Dakota	59	—	—	—	59	8	—
Tennessee[e]	—	—	—	240	240	—	6
Texas	8,181	—	—	16,000	24,181	117	231
Utah	—	—	—	—	—	—	—
Vermont	1,162	—	—	1,162	1,162	104	104
Virginia	441	—	—	441	441	17	17
Washington	721	—	—	721	721	34	34
West Virginia	928	—	—	928	928	104	104
Wisconsin	7,048	—	—	3,971	11,019	272	153
Wyoming	—	—	—	—	—	—	—

(Last column values: New Hampshire 3; New Jersey 320; New York 491; North Carolina 228; North Dakota 11; Ohio 184; Oklahoma 12; Oregon 178; Pennsylvania 555; Rhode Island 62; South Carolina 324; South Dakota 8; Tennessee 6; Texas 348; Vermont 104; Virginia 17; Washington 34; West Virginia 104; Wisconsin 425)

Note: Table does not include aid to proprietary institutions, which is provided under student-aid programs in a few states; also excluded is aid for construction. Includes minor programs, such as aid for orphan children of veterans, in certain states.

[a] FTE = number of full-time equivalent students in private higher education.

[b] Alaska's program of aid to students in private institutions has been discontinued. In computing private FTE enrollment in Alaska, we have included Inupiat College, although its enrollment is not reported to the U.S. National Center for Education Statistics.

[c] California has an authorized program for contracts with private medical schools, which was funded in 1975-76 but not in 1976-77 because of questions about a possible conflict with the state constitution.

[d] New Hampshire and New Mexico had no student-aid programs in 1975-76, but initiated student incentive grant programs that aid students in both public and private institutions in 1976-77.

[e] Tennessee's student aid program was not funded in 1975-76 but was funded in 1976-77.

Sources: Carnegie Council survey; Education Commission of the States (annual); and Boyd (1975 and 1977). In general, where amounts reported in these sources differ, we have used those reported in the Carnegie Council survey.

Table 16. State expenditures on student-aid programs and average award per student for students in public and private institutions, 1975-76 (expenditures in thousands)

| State | General grant and scholarship programs | | | | Other student-aid expenditures[a] | | Total expenditures | |
| | Public | | Private | | Public | Private | Public | Private |
	Expenditures	Average award	Expenditures	Average award				
United States	$221,839	$150	$310,427	$151	$5,297	$1,500	$227,136	$311,927
Alabama	439	—	70	—	—	—	439	70
Alaska	—	—	1,300[c]	1,368[b]	—	—	—	1,300
Arizona	—	—	—	—	—	—	—	—
Arkansas	343	222	118	128	—	—	343	118
California	15,818	580	42,030	2,239	—	—	15,818	42,030
Colorado	10,774	499	—	—	1,440	—	12,214	—
Connecticut	1,379	441	3,727	1,242	194	141	1,573	3,868
Delaware	—	—	9	—	9	9	9	9
Florida	2,964	1,100	1,634	1,150	33	—	2,997	1,634
Georgia	878	274	5,756	179	—	—	878	5,756
Hawaii	176	225	—	—	—	—	176	—
Idaho	96	589	20	571	—	—	96	20
Illinois	24,000	411	40,800	1,172	—	—	24,000	40,800
Indiana	7,083	536	8,291	804	—	—	7,083	8,291
Iowa	363	427	9,269	1,201	—	—	363	9,269
Kansas	420	467	3,005	908	—	—	420	3,005
Kentucky	801	231	849	476	—	—	801	849
Louisiana	495	406	64	405	—	—	495	64
Maine	50	25	382	637	—	—	50	382
Maryland	2,621	410	1,079	628	75	75	2,696	1,154
Massachusetts	3,280	328	9,010	910	250	400	3,530	9,410
Michigan	6,813	558	13,627	1,030	—	—	6,813	13,627
Minnesota	7,483	853	5,639	1,041	465	115	7,948	5,754
Mississippi	—	—	—	—	—	—	—	—
Missouri	931	233	2,852	634	—	—	931	2,852
Montana	79	267	—	—	—	—	79	—
Nebraska	—	—	—	—	—	—	—	—

State								
Nevada	—	—	—	—	—	—	—	—
New Hampshire	—	—	—	—	—	—	—	—
New Jersey	14,834	787	8,961	822	—	—	14,834	8,961
New Mexico	—	—	—	—	—	—	—	—
New York	56,813	303	73,950	556	—	—	56,813	73,950
North Carolina	540	775	8,661	200	59	128	599	8,789
North Dakota	223	300	20	303	—	—	223	20
Ohio	11,204	303	8,396	646	197	—	11,401	8,396
Oklahoma	428	310	207	214	—	—	428	207
Oregon	2,235	417	567	636	—	—	2,235	567
Pennsylvania	30,840	462	33,853	746	—	—	30,840	33,853
Rhode Island	1,067	750	985	750	55	15	1,122	1,000
South Carolina	—	—	7,351	1,280	193	—	193	7,382
South Dakota	169	185	59	181	193	31	169	59
Tennessee[c]	—	—	—	—	—	—	—	—
Texas	790	296	8,181	553	—	—	790	8,181
Utah	548	757	—	—	—	—	548	—
Vermont	1,566	429	1,162	1,273	—	—	1,566	1,162
Virginia	1,034	279	160	320	1,122	281	2,156	441
Washington	2,645	570	581	570	493	140	3,138	721
West Virginia	867	327	928	1,160	—	—	867	928
Wisconsin	8,750	527	6,883	782	712	165	9,462	—
Wyoming	—	—	—	—	—	—	—	7,048

Note: Includes only private nonprofit institutions; aid to students in proprietary schools, which is provided in a few states, is excluded. Appropriations for loan programs are not included. Total expenditures differ somewhat from those reported by Boyd (1975), because we include all programs except loans, while he includes only comprehensive undergraduate need-based programs. He also includes expenditures for students in proprietary schools, which we exclude. Our data include expenditures of federal State Student Incentive Grant funds allocated to states except where no state matching funds are appropriated and institutions must provide the matching funds.

[a] Minor programs include work-study programs, aid for health professions students, and other specialized aid programs. Where information was unavailable on the public-private distribution of funds, we have assumed that 50 percent went to students in private institutions.

[b] Alaska's tuition grant program, which provided grants to students in the state's two private colleges, was ruled contrary to the state constitution by the state's attorney general in June, 1976, and payments were halted by Governor Jay Hammond ("Alaska Aid," 1976). The number of recipients exceeded the number of enrolled students reported to the U.S. National Center for Education Statistics, because student aid was provided to students in Inupiat College (associated with Sheldon Jackson College), which is not listed by NCES.

[c] Tennessee has a student aid program, for which no appropriations were made in 1975-76, because the program was being challenged in court.

Sources: Carnegie Council survey; Boyd (1975); and Education Commission of the States (annual).

Table 17. Selected characteristics of state student-aid programs (other than loan and tuition waiver programs), 1976-77

State	Total number of programs	Characteristics of largest program aiding students in private institutions				
		Public-private	Eligibility— need, ability, etc.	Maximum award	Types of expenditures covered	Porta-bility
Alabama	1	Both	Need	No legal maximum; available funds divided equally among recipients	Tuition and fees	No
Alaska[a]	1	Private	All state residents attending private institutions	$1,850 (designed to eliminate public-private tuition /fee differences)	Tuition and fees	No
Arkansas	1	Both	Ability and need, freshmen only	$300	Tuition and fees	No
California	5	Both	Ability and need	$2,700	Tuition and fees	No
Connecticut	6	Both	Ability and need	$1,000	Tuition and fees	Yes
Florida	5	Both	Need	$1,200	Educational expenses	No
Georgia	2	Private	All state residents attending private institutions	Uniform grants of $500 for freshmen, $400 for other classes	Tuition	No
Idaho	2	Both	Need	$1,500	Educational expenses	No
Illinois	1	Both	Need	$1,500 or tuition and fees, whichever is less	Tuition and fees	No
Indiana	3	Both	Ability and need	$1,400 or tuition and fees, whichever is less	Tuition and fees	No
Iowa	3	Private	Need	$1,300, but cannot exceed tuition and fees less average amount that would be paid at a public institution	Tuition and fees	No

State						
Kansas	2	Private	Need	$1,000, but cannot exceed tuition and fees or financial need minus $450, whichever is less	Tuition and fees	No
Kentucky	2	Private	Need	Cannot exceed 50 percent of average state subsidy for students in public institutions	Tuition	No
Louisiana	1	Both	Ability and need	$500	Educational expenses	No
Maine	3	Private	Need	$900	Tuition	No
Maryland[b]	4	Both	Ability and need	$1,500	Educational expenses	No
Massachusetts	3	Both	Need	$900 in private institutions $600 in public out-of-state institutions $300 in public in-state institutions	Educational expenses	Yes
Michigan	2	Private	Need	$1,200 (undergraduate and graduate students)	Tuition	No
Minnesota[b]	5	Both	Ability and need	$1,000 but not more than one-half of applicant's financial need	Educational expenses	No
Missouri	1	Both	Need	$900 or one-half of tuition or calculated need, whichever is less	Tuition	No
New Hampshire	1	Both	Ability and need	$1,500 under full funding; $1,000 in 1976-77	Educational expenses	No
New Jersey	5	Both	Need	$1,000	Educational expenses	Yes[c]
New Mexico	1	Both	Ability and need	$1,500	Educational expenses	No

(continued)

Table 17. (*continued*)

State	Total number of programs	Public-private	Eligibility— need, ability, etc.	Maximum award	Types of expenditures covered	Portability
			Characteristics of largest program aiding students in private institutions			
New York	4	Both	Need	$1,500, but not more than tuition (undergraduates); $600 (graduate students)	Tuition	No
North Carolina	3	Private	All state residents attending private institutions	Uniform grant of $200 per student	Tuition	No
North Dakota	1	Both	Need; freshmen only	$500	Educational expenses	No
Ohio	2	Both	Need	$1,500	Tuition and fees	No
Oklahoma	2	Both	Need	$500, but not more than 50 percent of tuition and fees	Tuition and fees	No
Oregon	2	Both	Need	$1,000	Educational expenses	No
Pennsylvania	2	Both	Need	$1,200, but not more than 80 percent of tuition and fees, in state; $600 out of state	Tuition and fees	Yes
Rhode Island	3	Both	Ability and need	$1,000	Educational expenses	Yes
South Carolina	1	Private	Ability and need	$1,500	Tuition and fees	No
South Dakota	2	Both	Need	$200	Educational expenses	No
Tennessee	2	Both	Need	$1,200, but not to exceed tuition and fees or need	Tuition and fees	No
Texas	4	Private	Need	$600, or $1,200 if matched by State Student Incentive Grant funds	Tuition and fees, or educational expenses (SSIG)	No
Vermont	1	Both	Need	$1,650	Educational expenses	Yes

		Private[d]				No
Virginia	4		All state residents attending private institutions	Uniform grant of $400 per student	Tuition	No
Washington	2	Both	Need	$450	Educational expenses	No
West Virginia	1	Both	Ability and need	$1,243, but not more than tuition and fees	Tuition and fees	No
Wisconsin	6	Private	Need	$1,000	Tuition	No

[a] Alaska's program is no longer in operation.

[b] Maryland and Minnesota both have a second student-aid program that is nearly as large, in expenditures, as the program for which data are provided. Provisions are not greatly different, except that in Minnesota the second program is based on need alone.

[c] New Jersey imposes certain restrictions on portability.

[d] In effect for the first time in 1976-77.

Sources: Carnegie Council survey; Boyd (1975 and 1977); Education Commission of the States (annual); and McFarlane, Howard, and Chronister (1974).

Table 18. Estimated state student-aid payments per full-time resident undergraduate
enrolled in private institutions, 1975-76, by state
(arrayed in descending order of magnitude)

Payments per FTE	State	Payments per FTE	State
$1,710	Alaska[a]	$100	Rhode Island[b]
710	Vermont[a,b,c]	90	Kentucky
680	Illinois	70	Florida
590	California[d]	70	Washington
560	Wisconsin[a]	50	Arkansas
540	Iowa	20	Oklahoma
490	South Carolina	20	Virginia
480	Kansas	20	North Dakota
440	New York	20	South Dakota[b]
420	Indiana	10	Louisiana
420	Georgia	10	Alabama
400	Michigan	10	Idaho
390	Pennsylvania[b]	6	Delaware
370	North Carolina	0	Arizona
300	Minnesota	0	Colorado
280	New Jersey[a,b]	0	Hawaii
240	West Virginia	0	Mississippi
190	Ohio	0	Montana
190	Texas[a]	0	Nebraska
180	Connecticut	0	Nevada
150	Missouri	0	New Hampshire
150	Maine	0	New Mexico
140	Maryland	0	Tennessee
130	Massachusetts[b]	0	Utah
110	Oregon	0	Wyoming

Note: Payments per FTE are approximations only and have been rounded. Undergraduate FTE enrollment for 1975-76 was multiplied by the percentage of undergraduates in private institutions who were state residents, on the basis of the most recent year for which data on migration of students were available, 1972-73 (see Table 21).

[a] Data unavoidably include some payments to graduate students.

[b] Data include estimated payments to state residents attending out-of-state institutions.

[c] Data unavoidably include some payments to students in proprietary institutions.

[d] Payments to graduate students, for which we have separate data, were excluded.

Sources: Carnegie Council survey; U.S. National Center for Education Statistics (HEGIS) data; Education Commission of the States (1976b).

Table 19. State aid to students and institutions in private higher education, by type of program, 1975-76

State	Student financial aid		General support grants		Categorical grants and contracts		Indirect assistance
	Major programs	Minor programs	All private institutions	Selected private institutions	Specific programs	Construction	
Alabama	G			I	H		
Alaska	GL				H		
Arkansas	GL						
California	GFD	MW			HO	B	
Connecticut	GDL	M	I		S	B	
Delaware	L						
Florida	GL				H		
Georgia	GL				H		
Idaho	G						
Illinois	GL		I		HO	B	
Indiana	G						T
Iowa	G				H		
Kansas	G						
Kentucky[a]	GL	W	I				
Louisiana	GL		I		H		
Maine	GL						
Maryland	GLF	M	I			C	
Massachusetts	GL		I		H	B	
Michigan	GL		I		H	B	
Minnesota	GL				HO	B	
Missouri	G						T
New Hampshire[b]	L				H		
New Jersey	GDL		I		HS	B	
New Mexico[b]	L						
New York	GDL		I	I	HO	BC	
North Carolina	GL	H			H		

State						
North Dakota[c]	G	L		HO		
Ohio	GL				B	
Oklahoma	GL					
Oregon	GL		I			
Pennsylvania	GL	H	I	SO		
Rhode Island	GL	H		HO		
South Carolina	GL	LM		O	B	P
South Dakota[c]	G					
Tennessee[d]	GL	L		H		
Texas	GL			H		
Vermont	GL					
Virginia	GL	HM			BC	
Washington	G	W				
West Virginia	G					
Wisconsin	GDL	M		H		T

Key to symbols and abbreviations

B = Bond-issuing authority (tax exempt)	G = Grants for undergraduates	O = Other
C = Grants or loans for construction	H = Health professions	P = State purchasing office privileges
D = Aid to disadvantaged students	I = Institutional support	S = Services for disadvantaged students
F = Fellowships for graduate students	L = Loan programs	T = Tax credits or exemptions
or for selected professional fields	M = Student aid for specialized groups	W = Work-study programs

Note: Funds provided by states to assist or subsidize students pursuing specialized graduate or professional programs in other states, either directly, as in Delaware, or through a regional association (New England Board of Higher Education, Southern Regional Education Board, or Western Interstate Commission for Higher Education) are not included, because they do not assist private institutions in the state providing the funds. However, where the state funds are provided to assist an in-state institution but are administered through a regional association (SREB), as in the case of capitation payments by the State of Georgia for Emory University School of Medicine, they are included.

a Amount provided by Kentucky for a federal-state summer work-study program not available and therefore not indicated in Table 15.

b New Hampshire and New Mexico added student incentive grant programs in 1976-77.

c Loan programs in North Dakota, South Dakota, and Tennessee are for selected health professions students only.

d No state funds were appropriated in Tennessee for its student grant program in 1975-76, but funds were provided in 1976-77.

Sources: Carnegie Council survey; Education Commission of the States (annual); Boyd (1975 and 1977).

Table 20. Estimated value of federal, state, and local tax exemptions for higher education, 1976-77 (dollars per full-time equivalent student)

Source of tax exemption	Revenue cost		
	Private Institutions	Public Institutions	Total
A. Federal, direct tax exemptions			
1. Deductibility of life-time constributions to educational institutions[a]	299	32	95
2. Deductibility of bequests to educational institutions	116	8	33
3. Unrealized capital gains on gifts and bequests to higher education	31	3	10
4. Parental personal exemptions and tax credits for students age 19 and over	124	76	87
5. Exclusion of scholarships and fellowships	57	18	27
6. Exclusion of GI bill benefits for higher education	21	24	23
7. Exclusion of student survivor benefits under social security	13	12	12
Total of A	660	172	287
B. Federal, indirect tax exemptions			
1. Deductibility of nonbusiness state and local taxes	15	162	128
2. Exclusion of interest on state and local bonds	8	66	52
Total of B	23	229	180
C. State and local tax exemptions			
1. Property tax exemptions[b]	639	363	428
Total of A and B	683	401	467
Total of A, B, and C	1,323	764	895

[a] Includes some gifts to primary and secondary schools.

[b] Property values in 1971-72 were increased 40 percent in order to adjust them to approximate 1976-77 values. The effective rate of property taxation was assumed to be 5 percent (the actual rate was 5.4 percent in 1971 and 5.2 percent in 1973). No allowance has been made for payments in lieu of taxes or for direct payments for certain services. See Nelson (forthcoming) for an estimate of the value of such payments by private institutions in 1971.

Sources: Sunley (forthcoming); U.S. Department of Health, Education, and Welfare (1974); U.S. Bureau of the Census (1973); and, for FTE enrollment, U.S. National Center for Education Statistics (1977c).

Table 21. Percent of total undergraduate enrollment with out-of-state residence
by state and control, fall, 1972

State	Public Institutions	Private Institutions
United States (50 states and District of Columbia)	6.2	36.3
Alabama	8.6	32.5
Alaska	7.9	5.8
Arizona	14.3	38.2
Arkansas	8.6	33.6
California	1.1	18.5
Colorado	21.8	69.6
Connecticut	4.6	44.5
Delaware	40.9	56.3
Florida	5.8	43.9
Georgia	11.0	40.1
Hawaii	4.1	28.7
Idaho	12.1	55.4
Illinois	1.3	21.1
Indiana	10.4	52.3
Iowa	10.5	41.2
Kansas	9.0	44.6
Kentucky	13.1	35.6
Louisiana	5.1	39.0
Maine	12.9	70.1
Maryland	10.9	40.4
Massachusetts	4.2	44.8
Michigan	4.2	22.9
Minnesota	5.3	38.1
Mississippi	7.4	19.0
Missouri	8.2	46.8
Montana	14.1	33.9
Nebraska	9.1	46.8
Nevada	12.6	69.2
New Hampshire	33.2	74.2
New Jersey	2.0	21.0
New Mexico	11.7	30.1
New York	1.0	22.2
North Carolina	10.7	44.6
North Dakota	12.6	29.3
Ohio	6.5	37.5
Oklahoma	6.0	36.5
Oregon	8.3	55.5

(continued)

Table 21. *(continued)*

State	Public Institutions	Private Institutions
Pennsylvania	4.4	31.4
Rhode Island	15.1	55.1
South Carolina	12.0	32.4
South Dakota	13.4	46.6
Tennessee	9.9	55.8
Texas	4.3	21.9
Utah	15.2	62.0
Vermont	35.0	83.0
Virginia	16.2	45.1
Washington	4.9	36.0
West Virginia	20.1	55.5
Wisconsin	7.3	44.2
Wyoming	17.5	—

Source: Education Commission of the States (1976b).

Table 22. Federal SSIG funds as a percentage of state funds for need-based undergraduate student aid, by state, 1976-77 (in rank order from low to high)

State	Percent	State	Percent
New York	2.0	Washington	28.9
Pennsylvania	2.7	Idaho	36.9
Illinois	3.2	Georgia	39.8
New Jersey	4.2	North Dakota	40.7
Vermont	4.2	Maryland	42.5
Iowa	4.5	Virginia	47.3
Minnesota	4.6	Tennessee	48.4
Indiana	4.9	South Dakota	48.5
Wisconsin	5.1	Arkansas	48.7
South Carolina	6.3	Alabama	50.0
Ohio	6.5	Delaware	50.0
ALL STATES	6.5	District of Columbia	50.0
Colorado	6.6	Hawaii	50.0
Michigan	7.5	Louisiana	50.0
Rhode Island	10.3	Mississippi	50.0
Connecticut	10.5	Montana	50.0
California	11.0	Nebraska	50.0
Massachusetts	11.5	New Hampshire	50.0
Kansas	11.9	New Mexico	50.0
West Virginia	15.4	North Carolina	50.0
Florida	17.9	Oklahoma	50.0
Texas	18.0	Utah	50.0
Missouri	19.8	Wyoming	50.0
Kentucky	19.9		
Oregon	19.9		
Maine	25.5		

Source: Boyd (1977, p. 11).

Technical Supplement A

Recent Behavior
of Enrollment
in the Private Sector

The relatively slow growth of enrollment in private, as compared with public, institutions is a familiar fact. The loss in the share of enrollment in private higher education has occurred throughout the period since 1950 and can be generally attributed to the vigorous development of low-cost public higher education in virtually all of the states (See Figure 4). During the 1950s and much of the 1960s, however, the loss of the share of total enrollment in private higher education did not give rise to much concern, because both the public and private sectors were growing substantially, especially in the first half of the 1960s. In the 1970s, enrollment growth has slowed down in both the public and private sectors, in part as a result of the slowing growth of the traditional college-age population (Table 23). Since both sectors expect a decline in the size of the traditional college-age population in the 1980s, there are widespread fears that many private institutions will not survive in the atmosphere of intensified competition for students that is likely to prevail.

From 1963 to 1970, the less selective private institutions tended to gain enrollment more rapidly than the more selective groups

Table 23. **Total enrollment and enrollment in private institutions, by type
and by state, 1963, 1970, and 1975 (numbers in thousands)**

State and type of institution	1963	1970	1975	Annual average rate of change[a] 1963-70	1970-75
United States					
Total enrollment	4,765.0	8,548.3	11,148.0	8.7%	5.5%
Private institutions	1,672.5	2,128.2	2,350.4	3.1	2.0
Research universities I	255.5	252.5	260.3	-0.2	0.6
Research universities II	121.2	108.6	115.3	-1.5	1.2
Other universities	214.1	285.1	293.8	4.2	0.6
Comprehensive universities and colleges	390.2	520.3	555.2	4.2	1.3
Liberal arts colleges I	139.7	176.7	190.2	3.4	1.5
Liberal arts colleges II	343.6	473.5	516.6	4.7	1.8
Two-year institutions	80.6	121.1	133.8	6.0	2.0
Specialized institutions	123.5	186.5	285.4	6.1	8.3
Maine					
Total enrollment	17.4	34.1	40.4	10.1	3.4
Private institutions	6.5	8.7	9.4	4.3	1.4
Liberal arts colleges I	3.0	3.7	4.3	3.1	3.1
Liberal arts colleges II	2.2	3.3	2.7	5.6	-3.6
Two-year institutions	0.2	0.1	0.4	-6.5	30.0
Specialized institutions	1.2	1.7	2.0	5.4	3.5
New Hampshire					
Total enrollment	16.6	29.4	41.0	8.5	6.9
Private institutions	7.2	13.4	16.8	9.3	4.6
Other universities	3.5	3.9	4.0	1.6	0.5
Liberal arts colleges II	3.7	7.5	8.6	10.6	2.7
Two-year institutions	—	0.5	0.7	—	7.1
Specialized institutions	0.1	1.5	3.5	10.8	18.6
Vermont					
Total enrollment	12.2	22.2	29.1	8.9	5.6
Private institutions	6.8	9.7	12.0	5.2	4.3
Comprehensive universities and colleges	1.2	1.4	1.7	2.8	3.4
Liberal arts colleges I	2.1	3.7	4.4	8.4	3.2
Liberal arts colleges II	2.4	3.1	4.5	3.8	7.9
Two-year institutions	1.1	1.4	1.1	3.7	5.8
Specialized institutions	—	—	0.3	—	—

(continued)

Table 23. (continued)

State and type of institution	1963	1970	1975	Annual average rate of change	
				1963-70	1970-75
Massachusetts					
Total enrollment	168.5	303.9	384.5	8.8	4.9
Private institutions	131.5	187.7	210.9	5.2	2.4
Research universities I	18.9	26.6	29.0	5.0	1.7
Research universities II	23.1	33.8	34.1	5.6	0.2
Other universities	32.8	49.9	52.5	6.2	1.0
Comprehensive universities and colleges	13.9	20.4	22.4	5.6	1.9
Liberal arts colleges I	15.2	16.4	16.7	1.1	0.3
Liberal arts colleges II	6.1	9.0	11.1	5.6	4.2
Two-year institutions	11.2	16.5	22.6	5.8	6.5
Specialized institutions	10.3	15.1	22.7	5.6	8.4
Rhode Island					
Total enrollment	25.0	45.9	64.5	9.0	7.0
Private institutions	12.8	20.4	32.2	6.9	9.6
Research universities II	4.5	5.8	6.8	3.7	3.3
Comprehensive universities and colleges	2.9	3.2	5.5	1.2	11.5
Liberal arts colleges II	1.6	5.6	5.0	19.8	-2.1
Specialized institutions	3.8	5.8	14.9	6.7	20.6
Connecticut					
Total enrollment	65.4	125.3	148.5	9.7	3.5
Private institutions	37.8	52.0	54.9	4.6	1.1
Research universities I	8.3	8.9	9.7	1.1	1.7
Comprehensive universities and colleges	20.6	31.2	33.6	6.2	1.5
Liberal arts colleges I	4.7	6.1	6.9	3.9	2.6
Liberal arts colleges II	1.2	1.4	1.4	2.9	0.0[b]
Two-year institutions	2.0	2.7	2.0	4.4	-5.4
Specialized institutions	1.2	1.6	1.2	4.8	-5.9
New York					
Total enrollment	487.4	790.7	1,005.1	7.2	4.9
Private institutions	263.0	335.3	391.2	3.5	3.1
Research universities I[c]	77.4	72.1	66.9	-1.0	-1.5
Research universities II	23.5	18.6	21.1	-2.9	2.6
Other universities	35.6	47.7	52.5	4.3	2.0
Comprehensive universities and colleges	73.6	108.0	114.8	5.6	1.2
Liberal arts colleges I	17.8	25.8	32.0	5.4	4.4
Liberal arts colleges II	11.3	18.3	25.4	7.1	6.8
Two-year institutions	9.8	11.6	20.1	2.5	8.1
Specialized institutions	14.0	33.2	58.5	13.1	12.0

Table 23. *(continued)*

State and type of institution	1963	1970	1975	Annual average rate of change	
				1963-70	1970-75
New Jersey					
Total enrollment	110.3	215.6	297.1	10.0	6.6
Private institutions	52.2	70.3	69.4	4.3	-0.3
Research universities I	4.4	5.2	6.0	2.4	2.9
Other universities	1.2	1.6	2.0	3.3	5.5
Comprehensive universities and colleges	34.9	46.6	42.7	4.2	-1.3
Liberal arts colleges I	1.4	1.5	1.4	0.6	-1.1
Liberal arts colleges II	4.7	5.9	5.8	3.2	-0.5
Two-year institutions	1.5	5.4	6.7	17.7	4.2
Specialized institutions	4.0	4.2	4.8	0.6	2.5
Pennsylvania					
Total enrollment	245.3	411.0	470.5	5.9	2.7
Private institutions[c]	179.7	177.0	183.1	-0.3	0.7
Research universities I	33.6	19.6	20.4	-7.4	0.8
Research universities II	31.4	5.0	4.8	-23.0	-0.5
Other universities	19.0	22.1	23.1	2.2	0.9
Comprehensive universities and colleges	37.8	50.3	51.3	4.2	0.4
Liberal arts colleges I	22.1	26.9	27.9	2.9	0.8
Liberal arts colleges II	19.9	27.7	26.5	4.9	-0.9
Two-year institutions	4.0	5.4	5.8	4.3	1.5
Specialized institutions	12.1	20.1	23.2	7.8	2.9
Ohio					
Total enrollment	219.6	376.3	436.1	8.3	3.0
Private institutions	76.4	95.2	99.1	3.7	0.8
Research universities I	10.7	9.5	8.7	-1.4	-1.7
Comprehensive universities and colleges	26.7	33.2	31.6	3.2	-1.0
Liberal arts colleges I	13.4	15.3	17.2	1.9	2.4
Liberal arts colleges II	19.1	25.2	23.0	4.0	-1.8
Two-year institutions	1.2	1.1	4.3	-1.5	30.6
Specialized institutions	5.2	10.8	14.3	10.9	5.7
Indiana					
Total enrollment	118.9	192.7	213.8	7.1	2.1
Private institutions	44.4	55.9	54.4	3.1	-0.5
Other universities	6.8	8.0	8.7	2.3	1.7
Comprehensive universities and colleges	18.7	22.5	21.5	2.7	-0.9
Liberal arts colleges I	3.9	5.4	4.8	4.8	-2.4
Liberal arts colleges II	11.8	16.0	14.5	4.4	-2.0
Two-year institutions	—	0.9	2.1	—	19.4
Specialized institutions	3.2	3.1	2.9	-0.4	-1.6

(continued)

Table 23. *(continued)*

State and type of institution	1963	1970	1975	Annual average rate of change	
				1963-70	1970-75
Illinois					
Total enrollment	250.3	452.1	584.1	7.7	5.3
Private institutions	117.9	136.5	139.6	2.1	0.4
Research universities I	25.2	25.0	24.9	-0.1	-0.1
Research universities II	7.6	7.6	6.5	0.0c	-3.0
Other universities	11.0	14.3	13.0	4.7	-1.8
Comprehensive universities and colleges	25.8	32.0	34.6	3.1	1.6
Liberal arts colleges I	10.4	12.2	11.7	2.3	-0.9
Liberal arts colleges II	17.9	23.4	25.1	3.9	1.4
Two-year institutions	5.2	8.5	7.3	7.4	-3.0
Specialized institutions	15.0	13.6	16.6	-1.4	4.1
Michigan					
Total enrollment	209.1	392.7	496.4	9.4	4.8
Private institutions	41.4	53.1	59.8	3.6	2.4
Comprehensive universities and colleges	13.6	12.9	12.2	-0.8	-1.0
Liberal arts colleges I	4.8	6.2	6.9	3.8	2.3
Liberal arts colleges II	11.0	17.5	18.8	6.9	1.4
Two-year institutions	2.7	3.3	4.7	3.1	7.5
Specialized institutions	9.4	13.2	17.0	5.1	5.2
Wisconsin					
Total enrollment	99.6	202.0	240.7	10.6	3.6
Private institutions	26.0	31.6	30.2	2.9	-1.0
Other universities	10.4	10.7	10.3	0.3	-0.7
Comprehensive universities	1.2	1.7	1.5	4.5	-2.7
Liberal arts colleges I	3.2	4.1	3.7	3.8	-2.0
Liberal arts colleges II	7.9	11.0	10.6	4.2	-0.7
Two-year institutions	0.7	0.6	0.9	-0.1	6.6
Specialized institutions	2.6	3.6	3.2	4.4	-2.3
Minnesota					
Total enrollment	96.9	160.8	184.8	7.5	2.8
Private institutions	22.3	30.2	36.1	3.9	3.6
Comprehensive universities and colleges	2.1	2.6	2.7	3.1	1.3
Liberal arts colleges I	7.1	9.5	9.9	3.7	0.9
Liberal arts colleges II	10.6	13.9	16.7	3.9	3.8
Two-year institutions	0.1	1.0	1.5	49.0	8.9
Specialized institutions	2.4	3.3	5.2	4.5	9.6

Table 23. *(continued)*

State and type of institution	1963	1970	1975	Annual average rate of change 1963-70	1970-75
Iowa					
Total enrollment	69.8	108.9	121.7	6.6	2.2
Private institutions	33.7	40.5	38.1	2.7	-1.2
Comprehensive universities and colleges	9.1	9.3	8.0	0.3	-2.0
Liberal arts colleges I	2.7	3.4	3.2	3.5	-1.0
Liberal arts colleges II	19.4	23.3	21.0	2.7	-2.0
Two-year institutions	2.0	3.4	2.1	8.2	-9.8
Specialized institutions	0.6	1.1	3.8	10.5	27.0
Missouri					
Total enrollment	103.4	183.9	223.1	8.6	3.9
Private institutions	45.3	51.4	64.9	1.8	4.8
Research universities I	12.6	11.1	11.4	-1.9	0.5
Other universities	9.7	9.4	9.6	-0.6	0.4
Comprehensive universities and colleges	3.2	4.9	10.5	5.9	16.6
Liberal arts colleges II	13.9	17.0	23.4	2.9	6.6
Two-year institutions	2.0	2.5	1.9	3.2	-5.5
Specialized institutions	3.9	6.7	8.3	8.0	4.5
North Dakota					
Total enrollment	17.8	31.5	29.7	8.5	-1.2
Private institutions	0.6	1.3	1.8	11.4	6.5
Liberal arts colleges II	0.5	1.2	1.4	11.4	2.9
Two-year institutions	0.1	0.1	0.4	10.8	28.4
South Dakota					
Total enrollment	17.3	30.6	30.3	7.4	-0.3
Private institutions	4.7	6.7	8.3	5.1	4.5
Comprehensive universities and colleges	1.7	2.2	2.2	3.8	0.6
Liberal arts colleges II	2.7	3.2	2.6	2.4	-4.1
Two-year institutions	0.4	0.4	0.4	0.6	2.4
Specialized institutions	—	1.0	3.1	—	25.2
Nebraska					
Total enrollment	41.0	66.9	74.7	7.2	2.2
Private institutions	10.9	15.5	13.5	5.2	-2.7
Comprehensive universities and colleges	4.6	5.8	5.9	3.5	0.3
Liberal arts colleges II	5.7	8.7	6.6	6.3	-5.5
Two-year institutions	0.3	0.3	0.3	3.1	1.6
Specialized institutions	0.4	0.6	0.6	8.2	0.6

(continued)

Table 23. *(continued)*

State and type of institution	1963	1970	1975	Annual average rate of change	
				1963-70	1970-75
Kansas					
Total enrollment	64.4	102.5	120.8	6.9	3.3
Private institutions	11.6	14.3	13.1	3.1	-1.7
Liberal arts colleges II	10.0	12.2	10.9	2.8	-2.2
Two-year institutions	1.4	1.8	1.7	3.5	-1.0
Specialized institutions	0.1	0.3	0.4	10.4	9.5
Delaware					
Total enrollment	10.8	25.3	32.4	13.0	5.1
Private institutions	1.8	4.1	5.3	12.6	5.3
Liberal arts colleges II	—	0.5	0.7	—	9.5
Two-year institutions	1.8	3.6	4.6	10.8	4.7
Maryland					
Total enrollment	76.3	149.6	205.6	10.1	6.6
Private institutions[d]	28.4	30.6	29.0	1.1	-1.1
Research universities I	9.0	9.7	10.1	1.7	0.8
Comprehensive universities and colleges	6.5	7.9	4.6	2.8	-10.0
Liberal arts colleges I	4.4	5.9	7.0	4.5	3.6
Liberal arts colleges II	4.5	3.6	2.8	-3.2	-4.4
Two-year institutions	0.2	0.4	1.3	7.2	29.8
Specialized institutions	3.8	3.2	3.2	-2.4	-0.4
Virginia					
Total enrollment	74.9	151.9	244.7	10.6	10.0
Private institutions	22.1	28.6	29.4	3.8	0.5
Comprehensive universities and colleges	5.5	7.6	7.1	4.7	-1.3
Liberal arts colleges I	4.5	5.5	5.4	3.1	-0.4
Liberal arts colleges II	7.6	11.3	14.4	5.9	5.0
Two-year institutions	3.6	3.2	1.2	-1.4	-18.4
Specialized institutions	1.0	1.0	1.4	0.5	6.6
West Virginia					
Total enrollment	36.1	63.2	78.6	8.3	4.5
Private institutions	8.3	11.8	10.5	5.2	-2.3
Comprehensive universities and colleges	1.4	1.8	1.8	4.0	0.2
Liberal arts colleges II	5.8	8.1	6.8	4.8	-3.5
Two-year institutions	1.1	1.7	1.6	6.9	-1.1
Specialized institutions	—	0.2	0.3	—	13.3

Table 23. *(continued)*

State and type of institution	1963	1970	1975	Annual average rate of change	
				1963-70	1970-75
North Carolina					
Total enrollment	93.0	171.9	251.8	9.2	7.9
Private institutions	40.5	47.6	50.5	2.3	1.2
Research universities I	6.5	7.7	9.2	2.6	3.5
Comprehensive universities and colleges	6.1	7.3	7.8	2.6	1.4
Liberal arts colleges I	1.5	1.6	1.9	0.7	4.1
Liberal arts colleges II	20.1	22.2	23.5	1.5	1.1
Two-year institutions	5.6	7.9	6.8	4.9	-2.8
Specialized institutions	0.7	0.9	1.3	2.8	7.4
South Carolina					
Total enrollment	36.5	69.5	133.0	10.3	13.9
Private institutions	14.9	21.8	25.3	5.5	3.1
Comprehensive universities and colleges	2.4	3.7	4.2	6.1	2.7
Liberal arts colleges I	1.6	2.0	2.7	3.7	6.1
Liberal arts colleges II	8.7	12.2	14.0	5.0	2.8
Two-year institutions	1.7	3.1	3.5	9.1	7.3
Specialized institutions	0.6	0.7	0.9	3.6	4.0
Georgia					
Total enrollment	62.3	126.5	173.6	8.3	6.5
Private institutions	18.7	24.2	31.0	3.7	5.1
Research universities II	4.7	5.3	7.2	1.6	6.2
Comprehensive universities and colleges	1.5	1.7	2.2	1.7	4.9
Liberal arts colleges I	0.7	0.7	0.6	-0.1	-4.0
Liberal arts colleges II	8.1	11.3	14.5	4.8	5.1
Two-year institutions	2.5	2.9	3.8	2.4	5.2
Specialized institutions	1.1	2.2	2.8	10.0	4.7
Florida					
Total enrollment	108.1	235.5	344.3	11.8	6.5
Private institutions	36.9	46.1	56.5	3.2	4.2
Research universities I	13.1	16.0	14.8	2.9	-1.6
Comprehensive universities and colleges	9.8	11.2	11.2	1.9	_b
Liberal arts colleges I	—	1.5	0.8	—	-11.1
Liberal arts colleges II	5.7	8.4	11.5	5.9	6.3
Two-year institutions	2.1	2.7	0.6	3.6	-26.2
Specialized institutions	6.2	6.2	17.6	_b	23.3

(continued)

Table 23. *(continued)*

State and type of institution	1963	1970	1975	Annual average rate of change 1963-70	1970-75
Kentucky					
Total enrollment	57.9	98.6	125.3	7.9	4.9
Private institutions	18.4	21.4	20.0	2.2	-1.3
Liberal arts colleges I	1.9	2.2	2.3	1.7	1.0
Liberal arts colleges II	13.3	15.1	12.8	1.8	-3.2
Two-year institutions	1.7	1.8	1.6	1.1	-2.0
Specialized institutions	1.5	2.3	3.3	6.3	7.2
Tennessee					
Total enrollment	77.3	135.1	181.4	8.3	6.1
Private institutions	26.4	36.2	41.9	4.6	3.0
Research universities I	4.4	6.4	7.0	5.5	1.9
Comprehensive universities and colleges	3.4	3.7	3.4	1.3	-1.5
Liberal arts colleges I	1.7	2.0	2.2	2.7	1.7
Liberal arts colleges II	14.5	20.2	21.9	4.9	1.6
Two-year institutions	1.3	1.9	2.0	5.3	0.4
Specialized institutions	1.2	1.9	5.4	7.0	22.7
Alabama					
Total enrollment	51.4	103.9	164.7	10.6	9.7
Private institutions	12.9	16.1	19.0	3.2	3.4
Comprehensive universities and colleges	4.7	5.6	7.2	2.4	5.1
Liberal arts colleges II	7.1	8.8	9.2	3.2	0.7
Two-year institutions	0.9	1.4	2.4	6.7	10.9
Specialized institutions	0.1	0.2	0.3	5.1	7.0
Mississippi					
Total enrollment	42.8	74.0	100.0	8.1	6.2
Private institutions	7.5	9.0	10.0	2.7	2.2
Comprehensive universities and colleges	1.8	2.4	3.0	4.0	4.6
Liberal arts colleges II	3.9	4.6	5.5	2.4	3.9
Two-year institutions	1.7	2.0	1.1	1.8	-10.5
Specialized institutions	0.1	0.1	0.4	2.0	37.5
Arkansas					
Total enrollment	33.2	52.0	65.5	6.6	4.7
Private institutions	5.4	8.4	9.4	6.5	2.2
Comprehensive universities and colleges	2.6	3.4	4.3	4.0	4.3
Liberal arts colleges II	2.3	3.7	4.1	7.1	1.8
Two-year institutions	0.5	1.3	0.8	14.9	-7.5
Specialized institutions	—	—	0.2	—	—

Table 23. *(continued)*

State and type of institution	1963	1970	1975	Annual average rate of change	
				1963-70	1970-75
Louisiana					
Total enrollment	69.8	120.7	153.2	8.1	4.9
Private institutions	16.2	19.6	21.2	2.8	1.5
Research universities II	7.5	8.5	9.1	1.8	1.5
Comprehensive universities and colleges	3.0	5.0	4.6	7.6	-1.5
Liberal arts colleges II	4.8	5.4	6.6	1.7	3.9
Two-year institutions	0.0^b	—	—	—	—
Specialized institutions	0.9	0.7	0.9	-2.9	2.8
Oklahoma					
Total enrollment	71.9	110.2	146.6	6.3	5.9
Private institutions	13.7	18.7	22.2	4.5	3.5
Other universities	5.3	6.4	6.5	2.8	0.4
Comprehensive universities and colleges	5.0	5.6	5.9	1.9	1.2
Liberal arts colleges II	2.1	4.0	6.2	9.7	9.1
Two-year institutions	1.3	2.8	3.5	11.1	4.8
Specialized institutions	0.0^b	—	0.1	—	—
Texas					
Total enrollment	237.2	442.2	624.4	9.3	7.1
Private institutions	55.8	76.7	82.4	4.7	1.4
Research universities II	2.2	3.1	3.6	5.0	3.2
Other universities	20.8	23.1	24.4	1.5	1.1
Comprehensive universities and colleges	13.4	17.3	18.2	3.7	1.0
Liberal arts colleges I	1.1	1.1	1.2	0.1	1.9
Liberal arts colleges II	13.3	20.9	24.5	6.7	3.3
Two-year institutions	2.6	6.1	1.6	13.0	-23.5
Specialized institutions	2.4	5.2	8.8	11.6	8.0
Montana					
Total enrollment	16.9	30.1	30.8	8.5	0.5
Private institutions	2.3	2.8	3.0	2.8	2.1
Comprehensive universities and colleges	1.1	1.2	1.2	1.3	0.6
Liberal arts colleges II	1.2	1.6	1.8	4.0	2.7
Idaho					
Total enrollment	17.5	34.6	39.1	10.3	2.5
Private institutions	3.4	7.5	7.8	12.0	0.7
Liberal arts colleges II	1.6	2.2	2.0	4.5	-2.5
Two-year institutions	1.7	5.3	5.8	17.0	2.0

(continued)

Table 23. *(continued)*

State and type of institution	1963	1970	1975	Annual average rate of change 1963-70	1970-75
Colorado					
Total enrollment	57.8	123.4	149.8	11.4	4.0
Private institutions	11.0	14.8	13.4	4.4	-2.0
Other universities	6.5	9.4	7.8	5.3	-3.7
Liberal arts colleges I	1.4	1.8	1.9	3.7	1.0
Liberal arts colleges II	2.9	3.4	2.9	2.2	-2.7
Specialized institutions	0.2	0.3	0.9	7.4	21.1
New Mexico					
Total enrollment	23.1	44.5	51.9	9.8	3.2
Private institutions	1.6	3.7	4.3	12.2	3.4
Comprehensive universities and colleges	0.6	2.0	3.0	18.2	8.3
Liberal arts colleges II	1.0	1.6	1.3	7.2	-4.0
Arizona					
Total enrollment	50.5	109.6	173.5	11.7	9.6
Private institutions	0.8	2.0	4.9	14.2	19.9
Liberal arts colleges II	0.5	1.2	1.2	12.5	0.8
Two-year institutions	—	—	0.2	—	—
Specialized institutions	0.3	0.8	3.5	17.3	34.0
Utah					
Total enrollment	47.0	83.0	87.3	8.5	1.0
Private institutions	18.3	33.4	30.8	9.0	-1.6
Other universities	15.4	29.1	27.2	9.5	-1.3
Liberal arts colleges II	1.4	2.2	2.1	6.8	-0.5
Two-year institutions	1.5	2.1	1.4	5.0	-7.5
Nevada					
Total enrollment	5.6	13.7	30.2	13.6	17.1
Private institutions	—	0.1	0.2	—	13.7
Liberal arts colleges II	—	0.1	0.2	—	13.7
Washington					
Total enrollment	87.9	183.5	227.2	11.1	4.4
Private institutions	18.5	20.8	24.6	1.7	3.4
Comprehensive universities and colleges	16.2	18.0	20.9	1.6	3.0
Liberal arts colleges I	0.9	1.1	1.1	2.5	0.0[b]
Liberal arts colleges II	1.4	1.7	2.0	2.8	2.9
Specialized institutions	—	—	0.6	—	—

Table 23. *(continued)*

State and type of institution	1963	1970	1975	Annual average rate of change	
				1963-70	1970-75
Oregon					
Total enrollment	57.3	122.2	145.3	11.4	3.5
Private institutions	12.0	13.7	15.5	2.0	2.5
Other universities	1.8	2.1	2.2	2.9	0.7
Comprehensive universities and colleges	2.6	3.9	4.7	5.8	3.8
Liberal arts colleges I	0.9	1.3	1.2	4.7	-2.0
Liberal arts colleges II	4.6	5.0	6.0	1.1	-0.1
Two-year institutions	1.5	0.4	0.4	-12.5	1.6
Specialized institutions	0.5	1.0	2.0	10.1	15.5
California					
Total enrollment	721.9	1,257.2	1,787.9	8.3	7.3
Private institutions	90.8	133.7	170.4	5.7	5.0
Research universities I	31.5	34.7	42.4	1.2	4.1
Other universities	4.7	9.0	8.6	9.6	-0.8
Comprehensive universities and colleges	15.2	27.9	37.0	9.0	5.8
Liberal arts colleges I	6.6	8.9	9.9	4.3	2.2
Liberal arts colleges II	21.7	35.9	48.2	7.4	13.2
Two-year institutions	0.5	0.9	2.1	8.3	19.2
Specialized institutions	10.6	16.5	22.2	6.6	6.0
Alaska					
Total enrollment	4.4	9.5	14.0	11.6	8.2
Private institutions	0.4	0.9	0.8	9.1	-3.0
Liberal arts colleges II	0.3	0.7	0.5	13.1	-7.6
Two-year institutions	0.1	0.2	0.3	2.3	8.2
Hawaii					
Total enrollment	13.6	35.3	46.7	14.6	5.8
Private institutions	0.6	2.3	3.4	21.5	8.2
Liberal arts colleges II	0.6	2.0	3.4	18.7	11.7
Two-year institutions	—	0.3	—	—	—

a Annual average rates of change are computed from unrounded data.

b Less than 0.05.

c Temple University and the University of Pittsburgh are classified as private institutions in 1963 and as public institutions in 1970 and 1975. State aid to these institutions was greatly increased in the latter half of the 1960s. The statutory colleges of Cornell University are classified as public institutions throughout.

d The University of Baltimore is classified as a private institution in 1963 and 1970 and as a public institution in 1975.

Source: Adapted from U.S. National Center for Education Statistics (HEGIS) data.

(Table 23)—research universities and the more selective liberal arts colleges (liberal arts colleges I). In fact, research universities lost enrollment from 1963 to 1970, but this finding is entirely attributable to the fact that the University of Pittsburgh and Temple University were classified as private institutions in 1963 and as public institutions in 1970 because state aid to these two institutions greatly increased in the latter part of the 1960s.[1] In the 1970s, the specialized institutions have shown the most rapid increase in enrollment among the private institutions. Because these institutions tend to cater to adults and to persons seeking occupationally-oriented programs of study, they have benefited from the trend toward greater participation of adults in higher education and from the shift away from liberal arts programs toward professional and occupational programs that have been major characteristics of the decade. The appearance of a less favorable job market for graduates of traditional college programs has, of course, been a decisive influence underlying these trends.

(Later, when we analyze characteristics of private institutions that experienced particularly pronounced gains or losses in enrollment, we shall achieve a better understanding of the differences in enrollment experience of the major types of private institutions. Let us turn, at this point, to a discussion of regional and state differences.)

Regional and State Differences

Variations in enrollment changes in higher education among the 50 states from 1970 to 1975 were extremely pronounced and were much less closely related to differences in rates of growth of the traditional college-age population—defined for this purpose as the population aged 18 to 24—than was the case in the 1960s. In a general analysis of enrollment changes based on multivariate regression analysis, we found that rates of increase in enrollment in the 50 states were inversely related to enrollment rates of persons aged 18 to 24 in 1970 and to high school graduation rates in 1970. In other words, the lower

[1] We begin this analysis of changes in enrollment for the various groups of institutions in the Carnegie Commission classification with the year 1963 because that is the first year for which we have been able to obtain HEGIS tapes from the U.S. National Center for Educational Statistics.

the college enrollment rate and the lower the high school graduation rate in a state in 1970, the higher the rate of increase in enrollment was likely to be from 1970 to 1975. Also favorable to pronounced enrollment increases were a high rate of net in-migration to a state and a high per capita income.

To what extent were differences in enrollment changes in private higher education influenced by relative rates of enrollment growth in the various states? Changes in enrollment in private institutions tended to vary with changes in total enrollment among the states. However, the relationship was considerably more consistent in terms of full-time equivalent enrollment in universities and four-year colleges than in terms of total enrollment in all types of institutions (Tables 24 and 25). There was an even more decisive and consistent relationship between overall enrollment state growth and the percentage of private universities and four-year colleges that lost 10 percent or more of their enrollment from 1970 to 1975 (Table 26). Institutions in states with low or negative overall enrollment changes were in an especially vulnerable position, and vice versa.

Somewhat surprisingly, although private institutions experiencing particularly pronounced growth tend to be located in large metropolitan areas, as we shall see, we found no significant relationship between the rate of change of enrollment in private institutions from 1970 to 1975 and the percentage of a state's populations in metropolitan areas (data not shown). We shall find that large metropolitan areas tended to include substantial numbers of both gainers and losers among private institutions.

The Vulnerability of a Large Private Sector

Noting that a few states with extremely small private sectors displayed a sharp rate of increase in private enrollment from 1970 to 1975, we here examine the relationship between enrollment changes in the private sector and the percentage of enrollment in private institutions in the various states in 1970 (Table 27). We find a significant inverse relationship if we eliminate the states in which the private share of enrollment was 40 percent or more in 1970—a group with highly variable enrollment changes in the 1970–75 period. In other words, the states with small private sectors in 1970 had particularly favorable environments for relatively pronounced in-

Table 24. Full-time equivalent enrollment in universities and four-year colleges, by state and control, 1970 and 1975 (numbers in thousands)

State	Public institutions			Private institutions			Total		
	1970	1975	Percentage change[a]	1970	1975	Percentage change[a]	1970	1975	Percentage change[a]
United States (50 states and District of Columbia)	3,376.2	3,784.3	12.1%	1,492.2	1,549.7	3.9%	4,868.4	5,333.9	9.6%
Alabama	57.5	75.9	31.9	13.3	14.9	11.9	70.8	90.7	28.1
Alaska	3.1	2.7	-12.0	0.5	0.4	-29.6	3.6	3.1	-14.7
Arizona	50.4	60.2	19.6	0.7	1.0	45.2	51.0	61.2	19.9
Arkansas	36.3	38.2	5.3	5.1	5.4	6.8	41.4	43.5	5.4
California	317.1	374.2	18.0	91.9	111.1	20.9	408.9	485.5	18.7
Colorado	71.7	78.5	9.5	12.9	10.8	-17.0	84.7	89.3	5.4
Connecticut	37.7	44.1	17.0	37.6	39.2	4.5	75.3	83.4	10.7
Delaware	13.1	16.6	26.6	0.4	0.5	14.3	13.5	17.1	26.3
Florida	68.5	84.4	23.2	30.9	31.7	2.8	99.4	116.1	16.8
Georgia	66.9	79.5	18.8	18.0	22.5	24.8	84.9	102.0	20.0
Hawaii	19.6	19.5	-0.5	1.3	2.0	57.4	20.9	21.5	3.1
Idaho	20.1	21.1	5.0	2.0	1.8	-13.2	22.2	22.9	3.3
Illinois	148.8	153.4	3.1	90.8	91.3	0.5	239.6	244.8	2.2
Indiana	96.3	100.8	4.6	43.0	41.0	-4.6	139.3	141.8	1.8
Iowa	46.5	48.2	3.7	30.5	27.2	-10.9	77.0	75.3	-2.1
Kansas	60.9	62.3	2.3	10.7	10.0	-6.7	71.6	72.3	1.0
Kentucky	56.9	66.1	16.1	15.0	12.7	-15.1	71.9	78.8	9.6
Louisiana	81.4	97.3	19.5	15.5	16.9	8.6	96.9	114.1	17.8
Maine	16.2	18.7	15.1	6.8	6.7	-1.1	23.0	25.4	10.3
Maryland	60.6	66.9	10.3	15.5	17.2	11.2	76.1	84.1	10.5
Massachusetts	56.2	73.9	31.4	126.6	132.0	4.3	182.8	205.9	12.6
Michigan	182.2	197.1	8.2	30.6	32.4	5.7	212.8	229.4	7.8
Minnesota	90.4	88.9	-1.7	24.5	27.4	12.2	114.9	116.3	1.2
Mississippi	37.7	45.1	19.4	6.1	6.9	12.4	43.9	52.0	18.4
Missouri	83.7	86.3	3.2	34.6	42.2	22.1	118.2	128.5	8.7
Montana	22.5	21.3	-5.4	2.5	2.4	-4.4	25.0	23.7	-5.3

State								
Nebraska	38.9	36.3	-5.4	11.5	11.0	-3.8	50.3	47.8	-5.0
Nevada	10.0	11.9	18.5	0.1	0.1	106.4	10.1	12.0	19.1
New Hampshire	13.3	15.7	17.8	9.4	10.6	12.4	22.7	26.3	15.5
New Jersey	67.2	91.4	36.0	44.2	42.8	-3.2	111.4	134.2	20.5
New Mexico	29.6	33.0	11.3	2.5	2.9	14.1	32.1	35.8	11.5
New York	180.5	214.9	19.1	228.9	231.9	1.3	409.4	446.8	9.1
North Carolina	13.6	93.3	26.7	37.3	40.2	8.0	110.9	133.6	20.5
North Dakota	21.2	18.7	-11.9	1.1	1.2	10.2	22.3	19.9	-10.8
Ohio	188.4	193.0	2.5	69.2	64.2	-7.2	257.5	257.2	-0.1
Oklahoma	67.9	69.7	2.6	12.9	15.2	17.7	80.9	84.9	5.0
Oregon	48.3	50.0	3.5	11.4	11.7	2.2	59.7	61.7	3.2
Pennsylvania	137.2	153.8	12.1	124.6	125.0	0.3	261.8	278.8	6.5
Rhode Island	15.8	17.2	9.1	12.6	14.3	13.7	28.4	31.5	11.1
South Carolina	29.7	45.6	53.2	17.1	19.1	11.9	46.8	64.7	38.2
South Dakota	19.3	17.5	-10.5	4.9	4.3	-11.2	24.2	21.6	-10.6
Tennessee	72.6	79.2	9.1	30.8	32.4	5.3	103.4	111.6	7.9
Texas	208.9	236.5	13.2	54.8	60.0	9.5	263.8	296.5	12.4
Utah	35.7	37.8	5.8	27.3	25.5	-6.8	63.1	63.3	0.3
Vermont	9.8	12.3	25.3	8.3	9.4	13.1	18.2	21.7	19.7
Virginia	73.0	99.2	35.9	22.0	21.5	-2.0	95.0	120.8	27.2
Washington	68.1	67.5	-0.8	17.9	20.6	14.9	86.0	88.1	2.4
West Virginia	40.2	41.8	4.0	8.9	7.5	-15.5	49.1	49.3	0.5
Wisconsin	112.3	113.4	-1.0	23.2	22.7	22.7	135.5	136.1	0.4
Wyoming	8.1	8.0	-1.0	0	0	0	8.1	8.0	-1.0

a Percentages are computed from unrounded data.

Source: Adapted from U.S. National Center for Education Statistics (HEGIS) data.

Table 25. Percentage changes in full-time equivalent enrollment in private
universities and four-year colleges by percentage changes in full-time
equivalent enrollment in all universities and four year colleges, by number
of states, 1970-1975

Percentage change—	Percentage change—total				
	-10.0 or more	-0.1 to -9.9	0.0 to 9.9	10.0 to 19.9	20.0 or more
-10.0 or more	2	1	3		
-0.1 to -9.9		3	5	2	1
0.0 to 9.9	1		7	7	
10.0 to 19.9			3	5	3
20.0 to 29.9			1	1	1
30.0 or more					
Average	-10.2	-5.8	0.4	+8.5	+12.2

Note: Arizona, Hawaii, and Nevada are omitted, because they had very small enrollment in private institutions in 1970, a modest increase in absolute terms from 1970 to 1975, and an *extremely* large increase in percentage terms; Wyoming is omitted because it has no private institutions.

Source: Table 24.

Table 26. Percentage of private institutions losing 10 percent or more of their
enrollment, 1970 to 1975, by annual average rate of change of total
enrollment, 1970 to 1975, by number of states

Percentage of institutions losing enrollment	Annual average rate of change in enrollment (percent)					
	-0.1 to -0.5	0.0 to 2.4	2.5 to 4.9	5.0 to 7.4	7.5 to 9.9	10.0 or more
0 to 9%			2	3	1	2
10 to 19			1	7		1
20 to 29			4	2		
30 to 39		2	6	2	3	
40 to 49			2	2		
50 to 59	1	2	2			
60 to 69	1	1				
70 or more				1		
Average (unweighted)	58.5	47.4	29.5	22.6	24.8	5.3

Note: Alaska, which had only one private institution, and Wyoming, which had none, are omitted.

Source: Adapted from U.S. National Center for Education Statistics (HEGIS) data.

Table 27. Average annual rate of change in enrollment in private institutions, 1970-1975, by percentage of state's enrollment in private institutions in 1970, by number of states

Rate of change in private enrollment	Percentage of state's enrollment in private institutions					
	0.1 to 9.9	10.0 to 14.9	15.0 to 19.9	20.0 to 29.9	30.0 to 39.9	40.0 and over
-0.1 to -3.9	1	1	2	3	2	
0.0 to 0.9			1	2	1	1
1.0 to 1.9			2	2		2
2.0 to 2.9	1	3	1			1
3.0 to 3.9	1	1	3	1	1	
4.0 to 4.9			1	2		1
5.0 to 5.9		1	2			1
6.0 to 6.9	1					
7.0 and over	3					1
Average	7.2	2.2	2.3	1.2	0.5	3.5

Source: Computed from data in Table 23.

creases in private enrollment in the subsequent years, and vice versa.

This relationship emerges much more sharply on the basis of an examination of the behavior of the private share of enrollment in all universities and four-year colleges from 1963 to 1970 and from 1970 to 1975 (Table 28). (We eliminate the two-year colleges from this analysis because enrollment in public two-year institutions rose spectacularly in virtually all states. We also eliminate specialized institutions, which tend to cluster around very large cities and are relatively unimportant in less urbanized states.) The data strongly suggests that the most pronounced losses in the private share have been in states with particularly large private sectors in 1963. Table 29 tests this relationship and shows that it was quite consistent and decisive. Evidently it is easier for the private sector to hold its share of enrollment when it is small or modest than when it is large. Clearly, of course, the sharp losses in the private share in such states as New York, New Jersey, Massachusetts, and Connecticut in the 1963-1970 period were largely explained by the belated development of strong public systems in those states. On the other hand, the comparative success of the private sector in holding its share where it was small or modest in 1963 suggests that there may be a fairly stable demand for private higher education within a modest proportion of all families

Table 28. Enrollment in private institutions as percentage of enrollment in all universities and four-year colleges, by region and state, 1963, 1970, and 1975

Region and state	1963	1970	1975	Percentage point change		
				1963-70	1970-75	1963-75
United States	35.2	30.8	28.6	-4.4	-2.2	-6.6
New England	65.8	55.0	53.5	-10.8	-2.5	-12.3
Maine	34.3	23.9	22.7	-10.4	-1.2	-11.6
New Hampshire	27.8	40.7	39.7	+12.9	-1.0	+11.9
Vermont	52.3	40.6	41.1	-11.7	+0.5	-11.2
Massachusetts	80.8	68.2	64.5	-12.6	-3.7	-16.3
Rhode Island	42.2	39.9	41.6	-2.3	+1.7	-0.6
Connecticut	57.0	49.8	47.6	-7.2	-2.2	-9.4
Middle Atlantic	67.3[a]	50.6	46.3	-16.7	-4.3	-21.0
New York	61.8	56.5	52.5	-5.3	-4.0	-9.3
New Jersey	47.8	38.5	30.1	-9.3	-8.4	-17.7
Pennsylvania	72.2[a]	46.7	44.5	-25.5	-2.2	-27.7
East North Central	34.3	26.6	25.0	-7.7	-1.6	-9.3
Ohio	33.0	27.1	25.4	-5.9	-1.7	-7.6
Indiana	38.7	30.4	28.3	-8.3	-2.1	-10.4
Illinois	52.0	39.3	37.9	-12.7	-1.4	-14.1
Michigan	18.6	14.4	13.6	-4.2	-0.8	-5.0
Wisconsin	25.7	17.5	16.2	-8.2	-1.3	-9.5
West North Central	31.4	24.5	24.0	-6.9	-0.5	-7.4
Minnesota	22.0	19.1	20.2	-2.9	+1.1	-1.8
Iowa	50.2	41.4	36.4	-8.8	-5.0	-13.8
Missouri	44.1	30.0	32.2	-14.1	+2.2	-11.9
North Dakota	3.6	4.6	6.0	+1.0	+1.4	+2.4
South Dakota	12.8	19.4	19.1	+6.6	-0.3	+6.3
Nebraska	26.3	23.7	20.8	-2.6	-2.9	-5.5
Kansas	17.8	14.8	12.2	-3.0	-2.6	-5.6
South Atlantic	40.0	30.9	27.0	-9.1	-3.9	-13.0
Delaware	0.0	2.5	3.3	+2.5	+0.8	+3.3
Maryland	32.0	22.1	22.6	-9.9	+0.5	-9.4
Virginia	25.6	25.9	16.3	+0.3	-9.6	-9.3
West Virginia	20.9	17.7	14.1	-3.2	-3.6	-6.8
North Carolina	39.8	31.8	27.6	-8.0	-4.2	-12.2
South Carolina	38.5	34.9	27.0	-3.6	-7.9	-11.5
Georgia	27.2	19.3	20.0	-7.9	+0.7	-7.2
Florida	46.1	31.4	24.3	-14.7	-7.1	-21.8
East South Central	27.0	21.1	17.9	-5.9	-3.2	-9.1
Kentucky	28.7	20.4	14.7	-8.3	-5.7	-14.0
Tennessee	31.9	27.0	24.5	-4.9	-2.5	-7.4
Alabama	23.7	17.8	14.8	-5.9	-3.0	-8.9
Mississippi	18.5	13.9	13.5	-4.6	-0.4	-5.0
West South Central	23.2	19.0	17.8	-4.2	-1.2	-5.4
Arkansas	15.8	15.3	15.2	-0.5	-0.1	-0.6
Louisiana	22.2	17.0	15.2	-5.2	-1.8	-7.0
Oklahoma	19.0	17.2	17.6	-1.8	+0.4	-1.4
Texas	26.1	20.9	19.1	-5.2	-1.8	-7.0

Table 28. *(continued)*

| Region and state | 1963 | 1970 | 1975 | Percentage point change | | |
				1963-70	1970-75	1963-75
Mountain	16.4	15.6	13.7	-0.8	-1.9	-2.7
Montana	14.1	10.3	11.3	-3.8	+1.0	-2.8
Idaho	10.9	8.5	6.7	-2.4	-1.8	-3.2
Wyoming	_b	_b	_b	—	—	—
Colorado	19.8	14.2	12.0	-5.6	-2.2	-7.8
New Mexico	7.3	9.2	9.8	-1.9	+0.6	-1.3
Arizona	1.3	1.8	1.7	+0.5	-0.1	+0.4
Utah	37.2	42.1	39.8	+4.9	-2.3	+2.6
Nevada	0.0	0.7	1.1	+0.7	+0.4	+1.1
Pacific	24.1	20.7	21.6	-3.4	+0.9	-2.5
Washington	28.1	21.1	23.4	-7.0	+2.3	-4.7
Oregon	23.0	19.1	17.4	-3.9	1.7	-5.6
California	24.6	21.5	22.3	-3.1	+0.8	-2.3
Alaska	7.4	12.3	6.7	+4.9	-5.6	-0.7
Hawaii	4.3	8.1	13.0	+3.8	+4.9	+8.7

[a] Temple University and the University of Pittsburgh are included among private institutions in 1963 and among public institutions in 1970 and 1975; they were reclassified as public institutions by NCES about 1967, following a large increase in financial support from the Pennsylvania state government.

[b] There are no private institutions in Wyoming.

Source: Adapted from U.S. National Center for Education Statistics (HEGIS) data.

Table 29. Change (in percentage points) in enrollment in private institutions as percentage of enrollment in all universities and four-year colleges, 1963 to 1975, by enrollment in private institutions as percentage of such enrollment in 1963, by state

| Change (in percentage points) | Share of Private Institutions in 1963 | | | | | |
	0.0 to 9.9	10.0 to 19.9	20.0 to 29.9	30.0 to 39.9	40.0 to 49.9	50.0 or more
+10.0 or more			1			
+0.1 to +9.9	5	1		1		
0.0 to -4.9	2	4	3		1	
-5.0 to -9.9		4	9	3		2
-10.0 to -14.9			1	4	1	3
-15.0 to -19.9					1	1
-20.0 or more					1	1
Average (unweighted)	+2.0	-2.8	-5.6	-8.4	-13.0	-14.5

Note: Wyoming, which has no private institutions, is omitted.

Source: Table 28.

in most states—although the exact proportion will vary with differences in income level among the states, differences in religious composition, and the like. Also, traditional preferences for institutions with a Catholic or fundamentalist Protestant association can be expected to become less prevalent with rising educational levels of parents.

Changes in the private share from 1970 to 1975 were not as closely related to the share in 1970; although there was a weak relationship (data not shown).

The private sector, of course, may be losing its *share* of enrollment in universities and four-year colleges while experiencing rising enrollment, especially where enrollment in the public sector is growing rapidly. When we investigated the relationship between the private share of enrollment in universities and four-year colleges in 1963 and rates of change in enrollment in these private institutions from 1963 to 1975, we did not find a consistent relationship (data not shown). However, it was apparent that enrollment in private universities and four-year colleges rose quite rapidly over this period in states in which private institutions attract large proportions of their students from other states—for example, in the New England states. Moreover, it seems reasonable to suppose that a large private sector may be especially vulnerable if it depends heavily on state residents for enrollment. Pursuing this line of reasoning, we investigated the relationship between the share of the private sector in universities and four-year colleges in 1963 and the rate of change in enrollment in these private institutions, *after eliminating all states with 40 percent of more of their enrollment in private institutions attributable to students from outside the state.* For this purpose, we used the 1972 NCES survey of student migration (Table 22).

The results were quite decisive (Table 30). The larger the private share in 1963, the smaller was the percentage change in enrollment in private universities and four-year colleges from 1963 to 1975. Thus, in states with large private sectors that are heavily dependent on enrollment of state residents, the private sector may be comparatively vulnerable both in terms of its share and in terms of its rate of increase.

It is probably no accident that the four states in the two columns farthest to the right in Table 30—Illinois, New Jersey, New York, and

Pennsylvania—had relatively large expenditures per full-time equivalent student for student aid and general direct support grants to private institutions (Table 15). In fact, suspecting that states that traditionally had large private sectors were spending relatively large amounts on aid to the private sector, we investigated the relationship between the private share in 1963 and the amount being spent per full-time equivalent student in 1975. Again, we found a consistent relationship when we eliminated states in which 40 percent of more of the students enrolled in private institutions were from outside the state (Table 31). Similarly, for this same group of states, we found that amounts spent tended to vary with the extent of the loss in the private share from 1963 to 1975 (Table 32).

Were the states that were spending rather heavily on aid to the private sector enabling their private sectors to hold their shares more successfully than states that were spending little? In view of the results shown by Table 30, we should not expect the answer to this question to be positive, and indeed it was not, but the relationship was not particularly consistent (Table 33). States that were spending little or nothing on aid to the private sector tended to be characterized by

Table 30. Percentage change in enrollment in private universities and four-year colleges, 1963 to 1975, by enrollment in private institutions as a percentage of enrollment in all universities and four-year colleges in 1963, by number of states—for all states in which less than 40 percent of enrollment in private institutions in 1972 was from outside the state

Percentage change in enrollment, 1963-75	Share of Private Institutions in 1963					
	0.0 to 9.9	10.0 to 19.9	20.0 to 29.9	30.0 to 39.9	40.0 to 49.9	50.0 and over
-0.1 to -9.9						1
0.0 to 9.9						
10.0 to 19.9				1		1
20.0 to 29.9		1	1		1	1
30.0 to 39.9		1	2			
40.0 to 49.9		1	2			
50.0 to 74.9	1	2		1		
75.0 to 99.9			1			
100.0 and over	4					
Average change	204.0	46.1	40.0	39.9	24.2	11.2

Source: Computed from data in Tables 23 and 28.

Table 31. Enrollment in private institutions as percentage of enrollment in all universities and four-year colleges, 1963, by aid to private higher education per full-time equivalent student in private institutions, 1975, by number of states—for all states in which less than 40 percent of enrollment in private institutions in 1972 was from outside the state

Aid per FTE (in dollars)	Private share in 1963 (percent)					
	0 to 9.9	10.0 to 19.9	20.0 to 29.9	30.0 to 39.9	40.0 to 49.9	50.0 or more
0	3	2				
1 to 24	2	2				
25 to 49			1			
50 to 74			1			
75 to 99			1			
100 to 149		1	1	1		
150 to 199						
200 to 249						
250 to 299			1		1	
300 or more		1	1	1		3
Average (unweighted)	2.80	75.67	145.33	210.00	219.00	401.33

Note: Includes only student aid and general institutional support; aid for special programs is excluded because it cannot be expected to have any relationship to overall private enrollment. Alaska, which provided an extraordinary amount of aid per FTE to its two private institutions, and Wyoming, which has no private institution, are omitted.

Source: Tables 28 and 36.

slight gains in the private share, whereas those that were spending $50 or more per FTE were typically losing, but there was no clear relationship between the amount spent and the extent of the loss. Nor did we find that there was any consistent relationship between the amount spent and the annual average rate of change in enrollment in private institutions from 1970 to 1975 (data not shown).

The Gainers and the Losers

Despite the comparatively slow growth of enrollment in private institutions, there were surprisingly large gains and losses in certain types of private institutions in individiual states (see Table 23).

We define a gainer as a private institution that experienced an enrollment of 50 percent or more from 1970 to 1975, or that had no enrollment (on the basis of NCES data) in 1970 but did have enrollment in 1975. A loser, on the other hand, is an institution that experienced an enrollment loss of 20 percent or more in the same period or had enrollment in 1970 but was not reported as having

Table 32. Change (in percentage points) in enrollment in private
institutions as percentage of enrollment in all universities and four-year colleges,
1963 to 1975, by aid to private higher education per full-time equivalent student
in private institutions, 1975, by number of states—for states in which less than
40 percent of enrollment in private institutions in 1972 was from outside the state

Aid per FTE (in dollars)	Change in private share					
	+0.1 or more	0.0 to -4.9	-5.0 to -7.4	-7.5 to -9.9	-10.0 to -14.9	-15.0 or more
0	2	2	1			
1 to 24	1	1				
25 to 49		1				
50 to 74					1	
75 to 99			1			
100 to 149			1	2		
150 to 199						
200 to 249		1				
250 to 299						1
300 or more		1	1	1	2	1
Average (unweighted)	2.75	104.00	130.00	220.67	266.00	312.50

Note: Includes only student aid and general institutional support; aid for special programs is excluded because it cannot be expected to have any relationship to overall private enrollment. Alaska, which provided an extraordinary amount of aid per FTE to its two private institutions, and Wyoming, which has no private institution, are omitted.

Source: Tables 28 and 36.

Table 33. Aid to private higher education per student in private institutions,
1975, by change (in percentage points) in enrollment in private institutions as a
percentage of enrollment in all universities and four-year colleges, 1970, to 1975,
by number of states—for states in which less than 40 percent of enrollment in private
institutions in 1972 was from outside the state

Change in share of private institutions	Aid per FTE (in dollars)					
	0	1 to 49	50 to 99	100 to 199	200 to 299	300 or more
+0.1 or more	3	4			1	1
-0.1 to -2.4	1	1	1	2		3
-2.5 to -4.9				1		1
-5.0 to -7.4			1			
-7.5 to -9.9					1	1
Average (unweighted)	+1.5	+0.9	-3.8	-2.2	-3.7	-2.6

Note: Includes only student aid and general institutional support; aid for special programs is excluded, because it cannot be expected to have any relationship to overall private enrollment. Alaska, which provided an extraordinary amount of aid to its two private institutions, and Wyoming, which has no private institution, are omitted.

Sources: Tables 28 and 36.

enrollment in 1975. Our reasoning is that a gain of 50 percent or more in a period of very slow enrollment growth in private higher education is an unexpected phenomenon that calls for explanation. Institutions experiencing such pronounced gains might conceivably have something in common with new institutions that were attracting students. A loss of 20 percent or more, however, is substantial enough to force drastic readjustment and may perhaps be a forerunner of a situation that will force the institution out of existence. Hence our linkage of institutions with large enrollment declines and those that went out of existence.

The first thing to be noted is the large number of institutions in both categories. In all, 409 institutions among a total of 1,584 private institutions in 1975, or about 25 percent, were gainers. The population of losers included 314 institutions, or about 20 percent of the 1,505 private institutions that had existed in 1970[2]. These figures suggest an enormous amount of movement and change, despite the sluggish overall behavior of enrollment in private higher education during the period.

Secondly, the institutions were by no means evenly distributed among Carnegie categories (Figure 11). In the population of gainers, there were no universities, a sprinkling of Comprehensive Universities and Colleges (many of them former Liberal Arts Colleges II), very few Liberal Arts Colleges I, and very large numbers of Liberal Arts Colleges II, two-year institutions, and specialized institutions. Strikingly, however, the losers tended to be found in much the same categories as the gainers, and in the Liberal Arts II category, the number of losers substantially exceeded the number of gainers. Among two-year institutions, the number of gainers and losers was almost the same, while among specialized institutions, the number of gainers greatly exceeded the number of losers.

These shifts tended to favor occupationally and professionally oriented institutions over those that were more heavily concentrated on liberal arts programs. Not only was the excess of losers over

---

[2] The totals refer to the number of institutions in the 50 states and the District of Columbia; they do not include outlying areas.

Figure 11. Gainers and losers in private higher education, by type of institution, 1970 to 1975

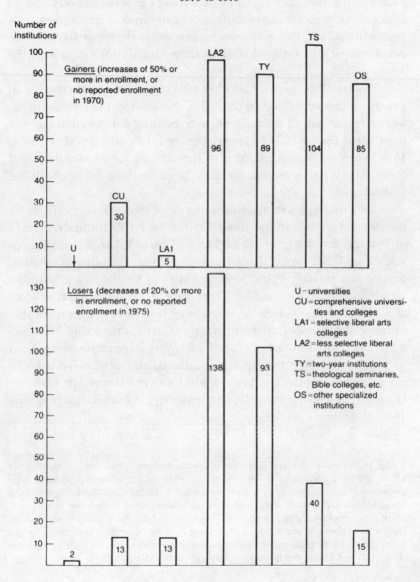

Source: Adapted from U.S. National Center for Education Statistics (HEGIS) data.

gainers greatest in the Liberal Arts II category, but the gainers far exceeded the losers among Comprehensive Universities and Colleges and among specialized institutions. Furthermore, among the two-year institutions, the gainers were considerably more likely to be occupationally or professionally oriented institutions than were the losers.

Figure 12 brings out another striking point about changes in private higher education in the 1970s. No less than 187 institutions, or nearly one-half of the gainers, were existing colleges that had not been listed by the U.S. National Center for Education Statistics in 1970, whereas the total number of new institutions was quite small (only 24). What accounts for this large increase in newly listed institutions?

Essentially, an institution must be accredited—or well on its way toward accreditation—to be listed in the NCES annual directory of institutions of higher education and included in its enrollment statistics.[3] What types of institutions gained eligibility for listing during this period? Table 34 shows that by far the largest number were specialized institutions. There were many theological schools and bible colleges—most of them very small—and a considerable number of other specialized institutions, which tended to be somewhat larger and , in fact, included a few very large institutions. Next in importance were two-year institutions, and here more than 50 percent were proprietary. The remainder were Liberal Arts Colleges II—most of them quite small and a majority associated with religious denominations.

[3] The 1975–76 directory specifies the following criteria for listing: 1. institutions accredited by a nationally recognized accrediting agency or approved by a state department of education or by a state university; 2. institutions that have attained a preaccredited status with designated nationally recognized accrediting agencies; 3. institutions not meeting requirement of criterion 1 or 2 if it can be confirmed that their credits have been and are accepted as coming from an accredited institution by not fewer than three institutions accredited by nationally recognized accrediting agencies (U.S. National Center for Education Statistics, 1976, p. ix).

Figure 12. Gainers and losers in private higher education, by status in 1975, 1970 to 1975

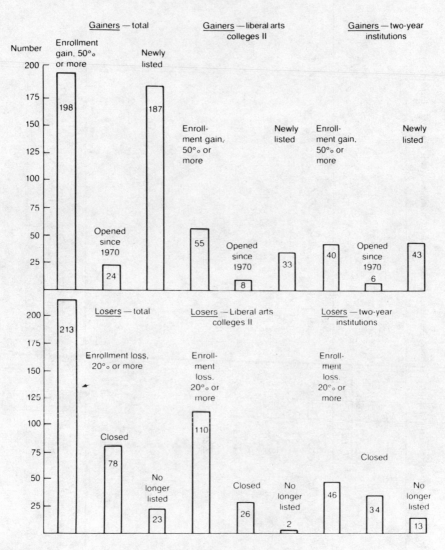

Source: Adapted from U.S. National Center for Education Statistics (HEGIS) data.

Table 34. Characteristics of institutions listed by National Center for Education Statistics in 1975 but not in 1970

Type of institution	Number of institutions	Percent of total in class	Enrollment Total	Enrollment Average	Adjusted rate of growth[a]	Independent non-profit	Religious	Adjusted religious[b]	Proprietary	Established before World War II	In larger metropolitan area
Total	187	10.9%	67,737	389	2.0 / 1.0	56.3%	27.6%	52.9%	16.1%	35.6%	87.4%
Liberal arts colleges II	33	4.8	8,873	329	1.6 / 1.2	59.3	40.7	55.6	–	22.2	77.8
Two-year institutions	43	17.4	26,614	619	1.8 / -2.6	30.2	16.3	16.3	53.5	53.5	76.7
Specialized institutions	111	23.2	82,250	336	7.9 / 5.3	66.4	28.8	67.3	4.8	31.7	94.2
Theological schools, Bible schools, etc.	64	23.5	11,089	182	7.0 / 3.3	52.5	47.5	100.0	–	27.9	93.4
Other specialized institutions	47	21.1	21,161	492	8.2 / 6.0	85.9	2.3	20.9	11.6	37.2	95.3

[a] The upper figure is the annual average rate of growth indicated by U.S. National Center for Education Statistics data for 1970 and 1975; the lower figure is the adjusted rate of growth obtained after excluding "newly listed" institutions (those that existed in 1970 but were not listed by NCES in that year).

[b] Adjusted to include institutions with a religious association that are officially classified as "independent nonprofit."

Source: Adapted from U.S. National Center for Education Statistics (HEGIS) data.

We need not search very hard to find plausible reasons for this large increase in the number of accredited institutions. Both federal and state student-aid expenditures have increased greatly in the 1970s, and in general an institution must be accredited for its students to be eligible for aid. Furthermore, the federal Education Amendments of 1972 made students in accredited proprietary schools eligible for various types of federal student aid for the first time. And, by 1976, there were 20 states (including the District of Columbia) in which students enrolled in proprietary schools were eligible for at least some types of state grants or scholarships (Boyd, 1977, p. 15). Accreditation was a usual requirement. The Carnegie Council's survey of state student financial aid officers indicated that, in 1975, students in proprietary schools were eligible for aid under the major programs of 10 states, whereas in several other states it was only under certain minor programs that students in proprietary schools were eligible. But the 10 states included such large states as Massachusetts, New York, North Carolina, and Pennsylvania, as well as a number of smaller states. And, interestingly, 16 of the 28 newly listed proprietary institutions, or 57 percent—nearly all of them two-year institutions—were in New York State. Examples are the long-established Katharine Gibbs School for secretarial training, the Laboratory Institute of Merchandising, Sadie Brown's Collegiate Institute, and the Tobe-Coburn School of Fashion Careers.

Another important point to be made about these additions to the family of officially recognized private institutions is that the enrollment growth attributable to them was somewhat fictitious since they all had enrollment in 1970. Without them, the annual average rate of enrollment growth in private higher education from 1970 to 1975 would have been considerably smaller than the recorded statistics indicate. We have indicated the extent of the reduction in Table 34—from 2.0 to 1.0 percent for private higher education as a whole. In the two-year category, there would actually have been a loss of 2.6 percent a year rather than a gain of 2.0 percent in the absence of these newly listed institutions.

More than one-third of these newly listed schools were established before World War II, and many date back to the nineteenth century. The vast majority were located in large metropolitan areas, and this was particularly true of the specialized institutions, which tend to cluster around large cities.

Figure 13. Percentages of gainers and losers in private higher education with
selected characteristics, 1970 to 1975

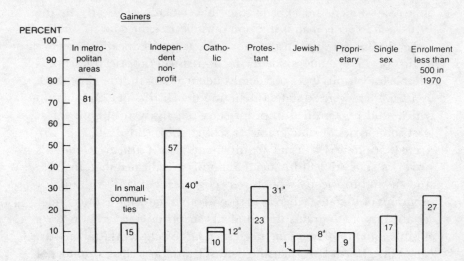

In recent years, many observers of developments in higher
education have speculated that private institutions located in relatively small communities were having difficulty maintaining their
enrollments. Our results tend to confirm this suspicion, though
perhaps not as decisively as might have been expected. The vast
majority of gainers (81 percent) were located in metropolitan areas
with 200,000 or more population, while only 15 percent were located
in small communities, which we have defined as those with
populations under 50,000 (Figure 13). Only a very small minority
(about 4 percent) were located in cities with populations from 50,000
to 200,000. A majority—but a considerably more modest majority (57
percent)—of the losers were also located in metropolitan areas, while
36 percent were in small communities.

Why were both gainers and losers more likely to be found in
large metropolitan areas? A study of the data suggests that competition is intense in large communities, not only between public and
private institutions but also among private institutions.

Gainers were more likely to be organized as independent
nonprofit institutions than were losers, but if we reallocate the

Figure 13. *(continued)*

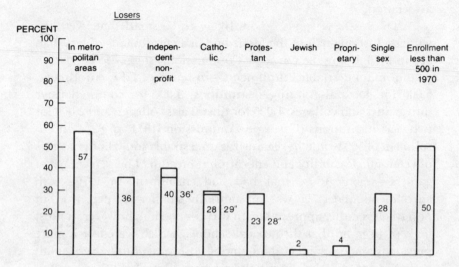

Losers

^aAdjusted to reallocate institutions with a religious association that are officially classified as independent nonprofit.

Source: Adapted from U.S. National Center for Education Statistics (HEGIS) data.

independent colleges with names strongly suggesting religious associations, we find that only 40 percent of the gainers and a slightly smaller percentage of losers were in the independent group. In recent years, many institutions with religious associations have reorganized as independent nonprofit institutions, for a variety of reasons, but probably particularly in order to remove doubts about eligibility for state aid.

Catholic colleges were much more likely to be found among losers than among gainers, and related to this was the fact that single-sex institutions were considerably more prevalent among the losers. A substantial proportion of single-sex institutions have tended to be Catholic. Protestant institutions were almost evenly represented among gainers and losers, while Jewish institutions were considerably more likely to be found among gainers. This last finding is largely explained by the considerable number of Jewish seminaries in New York City and Brooklyn that were not listed by NCES in 1970 but had appeared in the list by 1975. The great majority of these newly listed Jewish institutions are organized as independent nonprofit colleges, but their names clearly indicate their Jewish association.

The losers were also more likely to be small than were the gainers. Just one-half of the losers had had enrollments of less than 500 in 1970. Using the Carnegie Commission's suggestions relating to minimum desirable enrollments—in terms of FTE enrollment, 5,000 for doctoral-granting institutions, 5,000 for comprehensive universities and colleges, 1,000 for liberal arts colleges, and 2,000 for two-year institutions (Carnegie Commission, 1971, p. 82)—an enrollment of 500 would be regarded as undesirably small both in terms of economic feasibility and educational breadth. The percentage of gainers—among those that had had enrollment in 1970—with enrollments under 500 was substantially smaller (27 percent), but nevertheless rather appreciable. In this connection, however, it must be kept in mind that theological schools, which were much more prevalent among gainers than among losers, tend to be very small and were not included among the categories for which the Carnegie Commission made minimum enrollment suggestions.

Particular interest attaches to gainers and losers among less selective liberal arts colleges, in view of the very large number of losers and substantial number of gainers in this group. The gainers were much more likely than the losers to be in metropolitan areas and much less likely to be in small communities (Figure 14). Adjusting for institutions with names suggesting a religious association, we find that about 60 percent of the gainers and 70 percent of the losers had religious associations. Among these colleges with a religious orientation, protestant colleges accounted for well over half of the gainers and for slightly more than half of the losers. Catholic colleges, however, tended to be considerably more numerous among the losers than among the gainers, and, again, single-sex institutions were relatively more prevalent among the losers than among the gainers. About one-half of the losers had enrollments of less than 500 in 1970, but, among the gainers with any enrollment in 1970, the proportion with enrollments under 500 was almost as large.

Figure 14. Percentages of gainers and losers among private less selective liberal arts colleges, with selected characteristics, 1970 to 1975

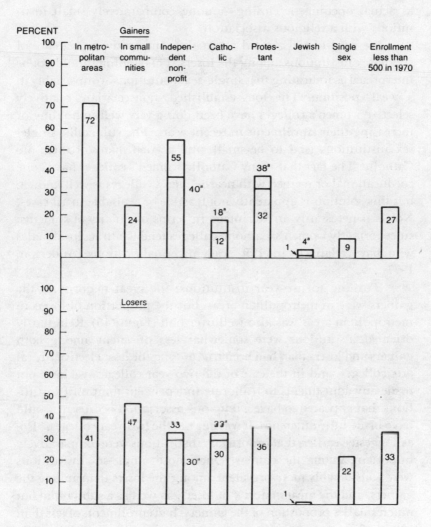

[a] Adjusted to reallocate institutions with a religious association that are officially classified as independent nonprofit.

Source: Adapted from U.S. National Center for Education Statistics (HEGIS) data.

All of this suggests that there is a considerable amount of turnover—including unusual losses or gains in enrollment, as well as actual opening or closing—among comparatively small institutions with a religious association.

We need to add a word about the comparative prevalence of single-sex institutions among the losers. This finding should not be interpreted as indicating that single-sex institutions are invariably in a weak position. The long-established, nonsectarian, relatively selective women's colleges have been doing very well in holding or increasing their enrollments in recent years. The vulnerable single-sex institutions tend to be small, and a good many of them are Catholic. The fact that many Catholic women's colleges have gone coeducational or merged with nearby men's colleges is well known, but this solution is apparently not feasible or available in all cases. Nor is it necessarily an advantage in terms of quality of students, since formerly women's Catholic colleges tend to attract local males who have relatively inferior academic qualifications (Anderson, 1977).

Turning to two-year institutions, the great majority of the gainers were in metropolitan areas, but the proportion of losers in metropolitan areas was also well over half (Figure 15). Religiously oriented institutions were somewhat less prevalent among both gainers and losers than had been true among the less selective liberal arts colleges; and in the case of the two-year colleges, we have not made any adjustments to reallocate independent nonprofit institutions that appeared to have a religious association because it would have made little difference. It was among the two-year colleges, also, as suggested earlier, that proprietary institutions were comparatively important among the gainers. Once more, single-sex institutions were considerably more prevalent among the losers than among the gainers, and the great majority of losers, as well as a substantial but much smaller proportion of the gainers, had enrollments of less than 500 in 1970.

Figure 15. Percentages of gainers and losers among private two-year institutions, with selected characteristics, 1970 to 1975

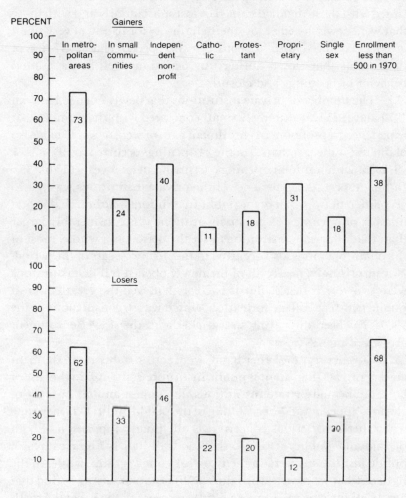

a Metropolitan areas have populations of 200,000 or more; we have defined small communities as those with less than 50,000. Thus, institutions located in communities of 50,000 to 200,000 are not included in these percentages.

Source: Adapted from U.S. National Center for Education Statistics (HEGIS) data.

Openings and Closures

Thus far, we have combined the institutions that actually opened or closed with those that had gained or lost substantially and with those that were newly listed or lost their eligibility for listing (a very small group). We need also to consider the special characteristics of institutions that closed during this period, as well as the annual behavior of openings and closures.

The number of private institutions that newly opened between 1970 and 1975 was extremely small compared with the number that experienced a pronounced enrollment gain or were newly listed. Also of interest is the fact that 20 of the 24 openings occurred in 1971–72 or 1972–73, with minimal openings occurring in later years (Table 35). In this respect, the experience of the private institutions was not so very different from that of the public institutions—although the total number of openings of public institutions was considerably larger than that of private institutions over the period as a whole, most of the public openings also occurred in the first two years of the period. Not surprisingly, nearly all of the newly opened public institutions were two-year colleges. But it is clear that even the great boom in public two-year college formation, which was so conspicuous in the 1960s, has been dwindling to a trickle with the slower enrollment growth of the 1970s.

Closures, on the other hand, were considerably more frequent among private than among public institutions, though in the case of both public and private institutions, the largest annual number of closures appeared at the beginning of the period, in 1971–72, at a time when there was serious concern over the financial position of both private and public institutions. Practically all of the closures of public institutions were in the two-year college group, while, in the light of what we have learned thus far, it is not surprising to find that nearly all the closures of private colleges were in the Liberal Arts II, two-year, and specialized categories.[4]

Can we draw different conclusions about the kinds of private institutions that are in trouble if we consider only those that have

---

[4] We have excluded from the closure data a few private institutions that were listed as closing during this period but that had no enrollment in 1970 and were not listed in the NCES directory for 1970–71.

Table 35. Number of institutions of higher education that opened or closed,
by type, control, and year of opening or closing, 1971-72 to 1975-76

Openings, closings, control and type	1971-72	1972-73	1973-74	1974-75	1975-76	1971-72 to 1975-76
Openings						
Public	24	15	10	8	2	59
Comprehensive universities and colleges	2	0	1	0	0	3
Liberal arts colleges I	0	0	0	0	0	0
Liberal arts colleges II	1	0	0	0	0	1
Two-year institutions	18	13	9	7	2	49
Specialized institutions	3	2	0	1	0	6
Private	13	7	2	2	0	24
Comprehensive universities and colleges	0	0	0	0	0	0
Liberal arts colleges I	0	0	0	1	0	0
Liberal arts colleges II	5	2	1	0	0	8
Two-year institutions	4	2	0	0	0	6
Specialized institutions	4	3	1	2	0	10
Closures						
Public	11	3	2	1	4	21
Comprehensive universities and colleges	0	0	0	0	0	0
Liberal arts colleges I	0	0	0	0	0	0
Liberal arts colleges II	1	0	0	0	0	1
Two-year institutions	10	3	2	1	4	20
Specialized institutions	0	0	0	0	0	0
Private	24	9	16	19	10	78
Comprehensive universities and colleges	0	0	0	0	0	0
Liberal arts colleges I	0	0	1	0	2	3
Liberal arts colleges II	4	2	9	6	6	27
Two-year institutions	14	5	5	8	1	33
Specialized institutions	6	2	1	5	1	15

Sources: U.S. National Center for Education Statistics annual directories of institutions of higher education (title varies).

closed, as contrasted with our total category of losers? The answer is a qualified yes. The institutions that actually closed were even more likely to have certain characteristics that we have found among the losers. In particular, they were more likely to be small; they were more likely to be Catholic; and they were more likely to be single-sex institutions (Figure 16). Relatively few were Protestant.

Among the liberal arts colleges that closed (combining the small number of Liberal Arts I with Liberal Arts II Colleges—just one-half were located in metropolitan areas, while 47 percent were in small communities (the same percentage that we found among Liberal Arts II losers). They were about equally divided between long-established institutions that dated from before World War II and more recently established colleges. Nearly one-half were Catholic and just one-half were single-sex institutions. The great majority of the single-sex institutions were Catholic, and thus 43 percent were *both* Catholic and single sex (chiefly women's colleges). Nearly one-fourth had enrollments of less than 200 in 1970, while 40 percent ranged from 200 to 499; in all, 63 percent had enrollments of less than 500. A sizable proportion (37 percent) had lost 20 percent or more of their enrollments from 1963 to 1970, while 30 percent had no enrollment in 1963 (in most cases having been established more recently than 1963). In other words, a substantial proportion of the closures were preceded by appreciable enrollment losses, while another group of institutions had apparently never become well established.

The two-year colleges that closed were somewhat more likely to have been in metropolitan areas than was the case with liberal arts colleges. Indeed, there appears to be a tendency for private two-year colleges to cluster in large cities, though to a less extreme extent than in the case of specialized institutions. Again, about one-half of the institutions had been established before World War II. Most of the institutions were either independent nonprofit or Catholic and were about equally divided between these two groups. The proportion of single-sex institutions was quite large (42 percent), though not quite as large as in the case of the liberal arts colleges. And the two-year colleges that closed were overwhelmingly small institutions, with no less than 58 percent having had enrollments of less than 200 in 1963. The proportion that had a previous history of losing enrollment was somewhat smaller than in the case of the liberal arts colleges, but a considerably larger percentage had had no enrollment in 1963 and thus apparently were relatively new institutions that had never become firmly established.

Figure 16. Percentages of private institutions closing, with selected characteristics, 1971–72 to 1975–76

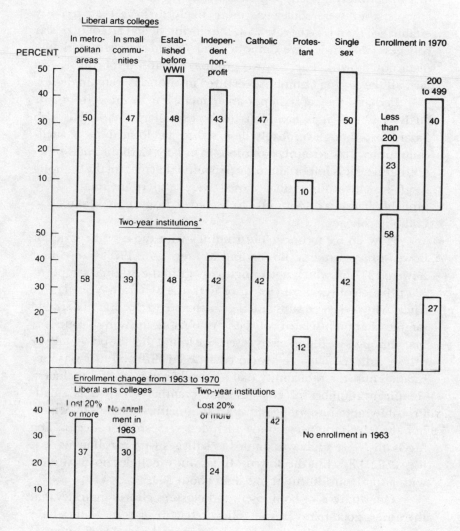

^a One of the two-year institutions was proprietary (not shown on the chart).
Source: Adapted from U.S. National Center for Education Statistics (HEGIS) data.

As for the specialized institutions that closed, they were overwhelmingly in metropolitan areas; they were chiefly theological schools; they were somewhat more likely to have been recently established than was the case with the closing liberal arts or two-year colleges; two-thirds were Catholic; and 73 percent were single-sex (data not shown). The last two groups overlapped, of course,—in fact, all the closing Catholic specialized institutions were single-sex.

Perhaps the most important conclusion to draw from this analysis is that it is hazardous to be extremely small. It is also hazardous, though probably less so, to be located in a small community. It is certainly hazardous to be both Catholic and single-sex, but here it is important to keep in mind that most of the Catholic single-sex institutions that closed were also quite small. They probably had less opportunity to become coeducational than large Catholic colleges.

How do we reconcile our findings with those of the series of Bowen-Minter studies (Bowen and Minter, 1975, 1976; Minter and Bowen, 1977) in which not a single college in the original sample of 100 private colleges had closed, or with the McGrath-Neese (1976) study, which showed substantial growth and no closures in a sizable sample of church-related colleges? An obvious answer, of course, is that although we found many losers, we found that the percentage of private colleges that actually closed between 1970 and 1975 was very small. Thus, the probability that a sample survey would include a significant number of colleges that eventually closed is small. Probably more important is the fact that neither the Bowen-Minter nor the McGrath-Neese study included very small colleges. The McGrath-Neese study was limited to colleges with enrollments of at least 250 FTE, while the Bowen-Minter study included no institution with a total enrollment of less than about 300.

Our analysis of both losers and closures clearly indicates that there are a good many private colleges that are marginal—they have always been small, they have been losing enrollment on a substantial scale, or they are newcomers that have not succeeded in becoming well established. The existence of these marginal institutions strengthens the arguments in favor of state policies that emphasize student aid over institutional aid.

Enrollment Changes in 1976

This analysis of enrollment changes has been based on data from 1970 to 1975 because the most recent HEGIS tape available is for enrollment in the fall of 1975. We need to add a few words about enrollment changes between 1975 and 1976, when, rather surprisingly, enrollment in public institutions declined slightly, while enrollment in private institutions increased somewhat, though at a smaller rate than the average rate of increase from 1970 to 1975 (Table 36). The main reason for this unaccustomed relationship between enrollment changes in public and private higher education was a sharp drop in enrollment of veterans, who were much more likely to be enrolled in public than in private institutions. In the fall of 1976, the Veteran's Administration reported that enrollment of veterans in higher education fell from 1,102 thousand in September 1975 to 727 thousand in September 1976, or 34 percent (Jacobson, 1976).

Despite the significance of the drop in enrollment of veterans in explaining the decline in enrollment in public higher education, there was no systematic relationship among the states between the change in enrollment in public institutions and the percentage of total enrollment consisting of veterans in 1975.

In the private sector, moreover, relationships between annual average rates of change from state to state in the 1970–1975 period and percentage changes from 1975 to 1976 were somewhat erratic. And, consistent with our findings for the 1970–1975 period, there was no relationship between amounts of state aid to private higher education per FTE in 1975 and enrollment changes from 1975 to 1976.

The slowing of enrollment growth in both public and private higher education from 1975 to 1976 probably reflected a combination of two influences—apart from the drop in enrollment of veterans—the declining rate of growth of the college-age population and the improvement in the job market between the fall of 1975 and the fall of 1976. The sharp increase in enrollment in the fall of 1975 had apparently been partly attributable to the extremely poor job market for high school graduates, but the overall unemployment rate was somewhat lower in the fall of 1976 than it had been a year earlier.

Table 36. Average annual rate of change of enrollment, 1970-1975,
rate of change, 1975-76, veterans as percentage of total enrollment, 1975,
and aid to private institutions per full-time equivalent enrollment, 1975,
by state and region

Region and state	Public Institutions			Private Institutions		
	Rate of change, 1970-75	Rate of change, 1975-76	Veterans as percent 1975	Rate of change, 1970-75	Rate of change, 1975-76	Aid to private per FTE, 1975
United States	6.5	-1.1	11.5	1.9	0.8	$231[a]
New England	6.8	-6.2	10.8	2.8	-0.7	58
Maine	4.1	-6.2	14.6	1.4	9.5	43
New Hampshire	8.7	-8.2	13.6	4.6	-1.0	0
Vermont	6.5	-0.6	3.6	4.3	-0.9	104
Massachusetts	8.5	-9.4	10.4	2.3	-0.5	56
Rhode Island	4.8	-2.8	16.0	9.6	-9.7	36
Connecticut	5.0	-2.2	8.9	1.1	2.2	108
Middle Atlantic	6.4	-5.6	8.8	1.3	1.4	384
New York	6.4	-9.2	9.2	1.9	1.6	442
New Jersey	9.4	-3.2	9.8	-0.2	1.3	291
Pennsylvania	4.2	0.3	7.4	0.7	1.0	535
East North Central	5.0	1.3	9.3	0.6	-0.2	275
Ohio	3.7	2.6	9.5	0.8	0.6	100
Indiana	3.1	4.2	8.1	-0.5	-0.4	178
Illinois	7.1	4.8	9.4	0.5	-0.1	428
Michigan	5.2	-2.9	10.4	2.4	-0.3	309
Wisconsin	4.3	-1.8	7.6	-1.0	0.1	272
West North Central	3.0	0.3	9.7	1.9	3.1	233
Minnesota	2.6	-0.7	7.9	3.6	6.9	263
Iowa	4.1	1.1	6.8	-1.1	-0.2	274
Missouri	3.6	-1.1	12.3	4.8	2.7	55
North Dakota	-1.5	2.0	8.9	6.5	14.1	11
South Dakota	-1.7	-1.3	13.1	4.4	2.8	8
Nebraska	3.5	4.8	10.3	-2.6	2.0	0
Kansas	4.1	0.7	9.7	-1.8	4.0	253
South Atlantic	9.3	-2.2	13.4	2.2	1.5	145
Delaware	5.1	-1.3	13.0	5.3	-10.3	3
Maryland	7.4	2.8	11.7	2.4	-1.3	265
Virginia	11.8	-4.7	12.5	0.5	2.6	17
West Virginia	5.8	2.7	8.8	-2.4	3.3	104
North Carolina	10.1	-3.2	14.7	1.2	3.5	183
South Carolina	17.7	-9.9	14.3	3.1	2.1	320
Georgia	6.9	-2.8	14.4	5.1	0.7	206
Florida	8.7	-0.4	14.1	4.2	7.0	33
East South Central	7.9	-1.2	12.9	2.1	3.8	12
Kentucky	6.4	0.3	13.5	-1.4	11.6	50
Tennessee	7.1	0.5	13.4	3.0	-0.4	0
Alabama	10.6	-4.5	14.8	3.4	1.6	120
Mississippi	6.7	-0.4	8.3	2.2	10.0	0

(continued)

Table 36. *(continued)*

	Public Institutions			Private Institutions		
Region and state	Rate of change, 1970-75	Rate of change, 1975-76	Veterans as percent 1975	Rate of change, 1970-75	Rate of change, 1975-76	Aid to private per FTE, 1975
West South Central	7.3	0.5	13.1	1.8	-2.7	88
Arkansas	5.2	4.4	11.8	2.2	1.1	13
Louisiana	5.5	0.9	9.7	1.5	-2.4	94
Oklahoma	6.3	0.3	13.4	3.5	-11.2	12
Texas	8.2	0.0[b]	13.9	1.4	-1.0	117
Mountain	5.8	1.4	13.6	0.1	-1.2	
Montana	0.4	-0.6	9.9	1.9	0.3	0
Idaho	2.9	1.8	10.2	0.8	-0.8	3
Wyoming	3.5	3.9	9.7	—	—	—
Colorado	4.7	-0.6	15.1	-2.0	0.1	0
New Mexico	3.1	7.2	14.0	3.4	-0.9	0
Arizona	9.4	1.8	15.8	20.0	-0.1	0
Utah	2.7	-3.6	9.7	-1.6	-2.3	0
Nevada	17.2	7.3	15.5	13.7	4.5	0
Pacific	6.9	0.6	13.7	4.6	-0.5	276
Washington	4.5	0.9	11.7	3.4	-7.0	34
Oregon	3.6	-5.3	10.0	2.5	1.6	177
California	7.6	0.8	14.1	5.0	0.4	314
Alaska	9.1	29.0	10.5	-3.0	-63.2	1,754
Hawaii	5.6	1.8	18.9	8.2	5.5	0

[a] Aid for special programs is omitted.

[b] Less than 0.05 percent.

Source: Adapted from U.S. National Center for Educational Statistics (1977c) and HEGIS data.

The slowing rate of growth of the college-age population and the actual decline anticipated in the early 1980s will undoubtedly make it more difficult for both public and private institutions to maintain their enrollments. A survey by Minter and Fadil (1977) of anticipated enrollment at independent colleges and universities—based on the sample of 100 private institutions used in the Bowen-Minter surveys—indicates the probability of no change in total headcount enrollment, but, somewhat surprisingly, an increase of about 5 percent in freshman applications, offset by a decline in incoming transfer students.

As our analysis of gainers and losers suggests, however, substantial variability in the enrollment experience of private institutions is likely to continue.

Technical Supplement B

A Short History of State Aid and Description of Selected Programs

From the time that the Massachusetts General Court in 1636 passed the legislation that led to the establishment of Harvard College, the colonies and later the states have had a primary role in establishing, financing, and encouraging institutions of higher education in the United States, both "public" and "private." During the colonial period and well into the nineteenth century, distinctions such as public versus private had little meaning (Whitehead, 1973), for colleges were viewed as serving public purposes: to combat ignorance and "barbarism," to instruct in citizenship, to train leaders of society such as teachers and the clergy, to support the religious and moral underpinnings thought necessary for civilized society, and to help men learn those things needful to run their world's affairs (Rudolph, 1962, p. 13).

Colonial and early state support for what we now call private institutions took various forms, for, as in other areas tinged with the public interest, such as banking and the transportation business, public and private forces joined in a partnership to provide needed services in a sparsely populated and capital-deficient nation. Permission to colleges to operate lotteries and land grants were the most popular forms of support by governments during the colonial and early national era, although direct grants to institutions were also common. For example, the General Court of Massachusetts provided the first funds for Harvard and made appropriations to the college on over one hundred occasions between 1636 and 1789. It has been estimated that, in the mid-eighteenth century, public support of existing colleges ran as high as 65 percent of their total operating income but that, during the greater part of the colonial period, it amounted to one-third to one-half of their operating income (Cheit and Lobman, forthcoming).

After the American Revolution and the formation of a new nation, increasing secularism led to the founding of publicly owned colleges, but a pattern of public-private partnership in education continued into the nineteenth century. Even Dartmouth, famous for the lawsuit that, in 1819, guaranteed the integrity of private colleges, continued to petition for state aid and received $200,000 from New Hampshire between 1893 and 1921 (Rudolph, 1962, p. 189).

State support of private higher education gradually decreased during the nineteenth century. Among the factors responsible for this decrease were: (1) other pressures on public funds, including pressures to support primary rather than higher education for a larger and more egalitarian population; (2) growing numbers of colleges, which discouraged support for all of them; (3) the decline of the "mixed corporation" in business, bringing new meaning to the words "public" and "private" in other spheres of activity (Cheit and Lobman, forthcoming); (4) the very close ties between most of the colleges founded in the early nineteenth century and religious denominations, in a nation with constitutional separation of church and state; and (5) the need to support those institutions wholly owned by states. Thus, institutions that had formerly been private but with substantial public support were rapidly becoming, in fact, private institutions.

The Morrill Land-Grant College Act of 1862 was a major stimulus to state support of more popularly oriented institutions, but, even so, the public-private distinction was not yet as clear as it became later on. Six states—Connecticut, Kentucky, New Hampshire, New Jersey, Oregon, and Rhode Island—designated private colleges as the recipients of their grants in support of higher education; Massachusetts divided state appropriations between public and private institutions; and two states—Indiana and New York—combined Morrill funds and private benefactions to support

new institutions (Purdue and Cornell). On the whole, however, after
the Civil War, state support went mostly to public colleges, whereas
private support became dominant in higher education as a whole.
Probably over two-thirds of operating income of all colleges and
universities in the last half of the nineteenth century came from
private sources, and 13 years after enactment of the Morrill Act,
public funds constituted only 10 percent of all current-fund income
of institutions of higher education.

Yet direct state support of private institutions (as well as
indirect support, such as through services provided or tax exemptions) never completely ceased. Through the first quarter of the
twentieth century, private colleges in at least five states—Maryland,
New Jersey, New York, Pennsylvania, and Vermont—were receiving
some public funds (Rudolph, 1962, p. 189).

By the middle of the twentieth century, however, the states
generally were concentrating their educational support on publicly
owned institutions, while private colleges and universities subsisted
on private benefactions, student tuition and fees, endowment
income, and, in the case of large research unviersities, funds from the
federal government. Yet Pennsylvania continued to provide basic
support to selected private institutions, New York continued to pay
private institutions to provide certain specified types of education,
and several states—including Maryland, New York, and Oregon—
awarded merit scholarships to be used at private institutions.

All this has changed in the last ten or fifteen years, as states have
come to perceive, as they did in the colonial era, the vital contribution
of the private sector and the necessity to support it in the interests of
public goals. The pronounced increase in the number of states with
programs of aid to private higher education since 1960 is indicated in
Table 37. In the case of need-based student-aid programs, the first
jump (from 5 to 23 states) came in the four-year period, 1968–1972;
and the second jump (from 27 to 37 states) in 1974–1976, after the
institution of the SSIG program by the federal government. By
1975–76, there were 12 states whose program of aid to private
institutions provided over $10 million a year; these were California,
Illinois, Iowa, Michigan, Minnesota, New Jersey, New York, North
Carolina, Ohio, Pennsylvania, Texas, and Wisconsin (see Table 15).

Pennsylvania is something of an exception to the general

statement that states moved away from support of private institutions during the century after the Civil War. Like so many other institutions we take for granted, the first college in Pennsylvania owed its inception to Benjamin Franklin, whose long-standing plans to open an academy in Philadelphia finally came to fruition in 1751 when the Academy and Charitable School opened; in 1755 it became a college with power to award degrees. Surviving by means of donations and public lotteries until the Revolution, it was a casualty of the political milieu following that war. After various organizational changes, the academy emerged as part of the University of Pennsylvania, chartered by the legislature in 1791 and containing in its charter a provision for public support, "the first direct contribution made by the Commonwealth of Pennsylvania to the cause of higher education" (Sack, 1963).

Table 37. Years in which programs of state aid to private higher education were first funded[a]

State	Competitive student aid[a]	Noncompetitive student aid (need-based grants)[a]	Institutional aid (capitation grants, contracts, etc.)
Alabama		1975	1963
Arkansas	1975	1975	
California	1956	1969	1975[b]
Connecticut	1964	1971	1969
Florida	1970	1972	1961
Georgia		1972	
Idaho	1976	1975	1975
Illinois	1958	1967	1971
Indiana	1966	1971	1971
Iowa	1966	1969	1972
Kansas	1963	1972	1975
Kentucky		1972	
Louisiana		1975	1973
Maine	1967	1975	
Maryland	c. 1825	1970	_c
Massachusetts	1958	1970	1973
Michigan	1964	1966	1972
Minnesota	1968	1969	1971
Missouri	1973	1975	
New Hampshire		1976	

(continued)

Table 37. *(continued)*

State	Competitive student aid[a]	Noncompetitive student aid (need-based grants)[a]	Institutional aid (capitation grants, contracts, etc.)
New Jersey	1959	1966	1972
New Mexico		1976	
New York	1913	1961	_[c]
North Carolina		1975	1971
North Dakota		1973	
Ohio		1970	1969
Oklahoma		1974	
Oregon	1935	1969	1971
Pennsylvania	1965	1969	_[c]
Rhode Island	1961[c]		
South Carolina		1975	1971
South Dakota		1974	
Tennessee		1972	1972
Texas		1971	1971
Vermont	1965	1970	1961
Virginia		1973	
Washington		1969	
West Virginia	1968[c]		
Wisconsin	1966	1965	1971

Note: In general, we give the year in which a program was first funded, rather than the year in which legislation was first enacted. In most cases, beginning dates are given only for programs initiated after 1960, because of the absence of satisfactory earlier data. States that are omitted from this table may have a program of student or institutional aid, but provide aid only for students in public institutions, require colleges to provide matching funds for federal SSIG allocations to the state, or have only a very minor and specialized program. See footnotes to Tables 15 to 17.

[a] The distinction between competitive and noncompetitive student aid is made in this table to bring out the point that many of the earliest programs were competitive, that is, based on ability rather than financial need. However, there are a number of state student-aid programs in which the distinction is not clearcut—both ability and need are considered. See, for example, the date in Table 17.

[b] California has an authorized program for contracts with private medical schools, which was funded in 1975-76 but not in 1976-77 because of questions about a possible conflict with the state constitution.

[c] The state has had a more or less continuous history of some form of aid to private institutions.

Sources: Carnegie Council survey; Boyd (1969 and annual); and Education Commission of the States (annual).

The new university had the state governor on its board of trustees but was otherwise a nonpublic institution and received no public funds during the remainder of the eighteenth century (except those due the old University of the State of Pennsylvania from confiscated estates, as provided in the 1779 charter). Similarly, other colleges chartered as private institutions by the state were also given initial grants of funds or income-generating lands, but subsequent aid depended on the ability of college officers to woo the legislature. Appropriations in the early nineteenth century were sporadic and haphazard, although up to 1837 approximately $250,000 had been given to Pennsylvania's 14 colleges and two universities, all private. In 1838 the Pennsylvania legislature set out a systematic program for financial aid to higher education institutions, but fiscal difficulties led to termination of aid before the ten-year plan had run its course, and little further aid was forthcoming until after the Civil War.

At that time the Agricultural College of Pennsylvania (later Pennsylvania State University) was designated as recipient of Morrill Act funds, while the state returned to its earlier practice of aiding selected institutions, especially those offering medical education and technical colleges. In 1895, the Commonwealth of Pennsylvania broadened the scope of support, appropriating $200,000 to the University of Pennsylvania for teacher training and facilities for graduate instruction. A less restrictive grant to Lehigh University in 1897 was followed in 1903 by aid to the University of Pennsylvania in legislation containing a clause setting out the policy that has continued to the present day; the appropriation for general maintenance, facilities construction, and equipment was to be used "as the trustees may deem best for the interests of the University" (Sack, 1963, p. 312). In 1919, four-year state scholarships, available for use at private institutions, were initiated. In that year, too, a court case involving Duquesne University limited state aid to private institutions to nonsectarian colleges and universities, as provided in the state constitution. Until 1965, state aid continued to take the form of annual subsidies for operating expenses to about 15 private, nonsectarian institutions. The number in this category is now 13, and nearly one-half are medical or health professions schools. A few of the others are specialized institutions.

In 1966, a statewide plan for higher education envisioned a "Commonwealth Segment," which would include Pennsylvania State University as well as two large urban universities, Temple and the University of Pittsburgh, which needed to reduce fees to approximately the level of those charged in state-owned institutions in order to survive and continue to serve students in the metropolitan areas. These and Lincoln University, added to the group in 1973, are the "state-related" universities, heavily subsidized by the state.

Pennsylvania thus offers a unique example of private-public partnership in providing educational opportunities for its citizens over a period of almost 200 years.

Turning to the present, we present below descriptions of programs to aid private institutions of higher education in five selected states: California, Georgia, Illinois, New York, and Pennsylvania.

California

Constitutional provisions. Several provisions of the California constitution explicitly forbid state aid to private institutions. For example, Article XIII, sec. 21, provides that no money shall be appropriated for the purpose or benefit of any institution not under the exclusive management and control of the state as a state institution, and Article IX, sec. 8, forbids state appropriations to support any sectarian or denominational school or any school not under the exclusive control of the officers of the public schools. However, the California courts have adopted what is known as the "child benefit theory"—the notion that a particular form of aid benefits the child or individual primarily and only incidentally aids the institution he or she attends. Thus, public subsidization of school busing for parochial school children has been held constitutional. However, the precise limitations of these constitutional provisions as they apply to higher education have never been tested in the courts.

Issuance of tax-exempt bonds for facilities construction at private institutions appears to be constitutional, as do the various programs for loans, scholarships, fellowships, and opportunity grants, since these primarily aid individuals and are not directed toward support of institutions.

Contracts. Under legislation passed in 1971, the state enters into contracts with independent medical schools to stimulate increases in their enrollment by providing $12,000 (minus federal capitation grants) for each additional student enrolled over enrollment in a base year. The total disbursement in 1975-76 was $1.5 million. The program was not funded in 1976-77, and its legality is in question.

Legislation passed in 1973 allows any school district or community college district in the state to contract with private institutions of higher education to provide vocational skill training.

Facilities. The California Educational Facilities Authority issues tax-exempt bonds for construction of facilities at private institutions of higher education.

Student aid. The State Scholarship Program is the principal means of assisting students in both public and private institutions; about half the awards go to students attending private colleges and universities. Awards up to $2,700 maximum are based on both ability and need, are limited to state residents for use at institutions within the state (no portability), and may be used only for tuition and fees. Administered by the State Scholarship and Loan Commission, awards totalled about $45 million in 1975-76 (rising to over $50 million in 1976-77), over three-fourths of which was used in private institutions with an average award of $2,172. Students in private institutions received a total of 16,873 awards, representing 19 percent of the undergraduate degree-credit students in those institutions.

Supplementing the State Scholarship Program are several more specialized programs. The College Opportunity Grant (COG) program is a need-based educational opportunity program for disadvantaged students, mainly intended for students attending public community colleges but not limited to them; about 12 percent of the awards in 1976-77 were used in private institutions. Funding in 1976-77 came to $15.7 million. The COG covers tuition and fees, books, subsistence, and personal expenses, with maxima for sophomores, juniors, and seniors of $2,700 tuition and $1,100 subsistence per year and a maximum for freshmen of tuition plus subsistence of $1,100. The number of grants that can be made is restricted to 6,825 new recipients each year (plus renewals), and 51 percent of the grants must be used in community colleges for the first year.

A fellowship program for graduate and professional students awards grants on the basis of ability and need for tuition and fees, up to a maximum of $2,500 for new awards and of $2,200 for renewals. About 50 percent of the grants in 1976–77 were used in private institutions, and funding amounted to $1.8 million.

The last major student assistance program consists of awards for two-year occupational education in both public and private institutions. The amount of the competitive awards is based on need, up to $2,000 for tuition and $500 for training-related costs. In 1975–76 the program was funded at slightly over $1 million ($1.4 million in 1976–77), with 59 percent of the awards and 86 percent of the funds used in private institutions. As with the other California student assistance programs, awards may be used at proprietary schools as well as at nonprofit private and public institutions.

A Tuition Grants Program was signed into law in 1974 to provide aid for students from middle-income families attending private colleges and universities, but it has never been funded.

Georgia

Constitutional Provisions. Although the Georgia constitution prohibits use of public money directly or indirectly to aid any sectarian institution, a 1972 constitutional amendment explicitly provides for state aid to Georgia citizens for educational purposes. In practice, the focus has been on the recipient of aid and not on the institution, so that conflict with the nonsectarian provision has been avoided.

Contracts and facilities. These mechanisms are not used in Georgia to aid or support private education institutions.

Student Aid. The Georgia Independent College Tuition Equalization Grant Program provides fixed sums for all state residents who are full-time undergraduate students in accredited private institutions within the state. Totalling $5.8 million in 1975–76, the program provides uniform grants of $400 per student each year in order to equalize somewhat the tuition gap between public and private institutions. Funds may not go to students at institutions that are "primarily sectarian" or that receive state funds under the 1970 Junior College Act; a further restriction is that students must be willing to work 10 hours a week.

Georgia Incentive Scholarships provide aid for first-time, full-time students who are Georgia residents in both public and private institutions, with grants up to $450. Begun as a program for freshmen, it was extended in 1976–77 through the junior year. Over 6,000 awards were made in 1976–77, of which 27 percent (29 percent of the dollars) were for students in private institutions. Funding totalled about $1.9 million.

Both of these programs are operated by the Georgia Higher Education Assistance Authority, which also operates a State Direct Student Loan Program. Grants under both programs must be used within the state of Georgia (no portability), and neither may be used at proprietary institutions.

Illinois

Constitutional provisions. The Illinois constitution, as it has been interpreted by the courts, poses no serious obstacles to public aid to private colleges in the state. There is a provision (Article VII, sec. 1) limiting use of public funds, property, and credit to public purposes, but the state supreme court has interpreted "public purposes" in a broad manner so that education of students in private institutions seems to fall in that realm.

In addition, Article X, sec. 3 prohibits payment of public funds to aid a sectarian purpose or to support an educational institution controlled by a religious denomination, but in 1917 the Illinois Supreme Court interpreted that section in a way that prompted the 1970 constitutional convention to adopt the original constitution's language, noting that it understood it to be no more restrictive than the First Amendment to the federal constitution. In 1973 it was interpreted in such a manner, with the court permitting use of public funds for transportation of parochial school pupils.

Contracts. There are no contract arrangements for support of private institutions.

Facilities. Private institutions may borrow money for construction of educational facilities through tax-free bonds issued by the Illinois Educational Facilities Authority, created in 1970.

Student aid. Under the Higher Education Student Assistance Law, grants are made on the basis of financial need for undergraduate state residents attending both public and private institutions within Illinois. This Monetary Award Program, totalling $64.8 million in 1975-76 (about $69.4 million in 1976-77), provides a maximum of $1,500 per year per student (or tuition and fees, whichever is less) for up to four years. In 1976, 38 percent of the grants and 64 percent of the funds went to students in private institutions. In 1975, there were 34,800 awards to students in private institutions in Illinois, representing 55 percent of FTE undergraduates in those institutions who are state residents, and the average award amounted to $1,172. While the average grant for students in private institutions is $1,000 less than that in the somewhat similar State Scholarship Program in California, Illinois made over twice as many grants in 1975-76 and to a much larger percentage of students in private institutions.

The Monetary Award Program is administered by the Illinois State Scholarship Commission, which also operates the Illinois Guaranteed Loan Program as well as other limited student-aid programs (e.g., POW/MIA dependents awards). None of the programs' grants may be used in institutions outside the state of Illinois or at proprietary institutions.

Institutional grants. The Illinois Financial Assistance Act for Nonpublic Institutions of Higher Learning provided capitation grants totalling $8.0 million in 1976-77. A private institution enrolling state residents receives $100 per student for lower-division and $200 per student for upper-division students, to be applied to tuition and fees.

Illinois also distributes grants for increased enrollment of state residents in medical, dental, nursing, allied health, and residency programs on both a formula and a project grant basis. Funds allocated to private health professions schools amounted to $11 million in 1975-76. Although the total amount available for private institutions was $21.3 million, part of the funds went to private hospitals affiliated with public health professions schools.

The state has a program of project grants for interinstitutional cooperation, available to both public and private institutions. Funds for this purpose came to $927,000 in 1976-77.

New York

Constitutional provisions. New York's constitution has a strong prohibition against aid to "any school or institution of learning wholly or in part under the direction or control of any religious denomination, or in which any denominational tenet or doctrine is taught" (Article 11, sec. 3). The constitution does, however, make a specific exception in order to allow busing of nonpublic school pupils. Some aid programs have been upheld, while others have been struck down by the courts.

At the higher education level, the section has been liberally interpreted, and the courts have ruled that mere affiliation or sharing of administrative control with a denomination will not disqualify an institution for state aid. Rather, the institution must be directed toward a religious end for aid to be entirely prohibited, so that in practice the situation is similar to that which obtains under the First Amendment to the federal constitution.

Facilities. New York aids private institutions in construction and maintenance of education facilities in at least three ways: (1) the Dormitory Authority provides tax-exempt bonds for residential and academic facilities construction; (2) deferred major maintenance loans aid private institutions in remodelling or restoring educational buildings; and (3) the Medical/Dental Capital Expansion Aid program provides aid for construction of medical and dental facilities. The program will be phased out in 1978-79, and funding has been decreasing in recent years: $8.3 million in 1975-76, $4.6 million in 1976-77, and $2.4 million for 1977-78.

Student aid. New York has a broad-based program of student aid: some parts are based on need; some are competitive; some are directed to students who are disadvantaged financially or academically (or both); and some aim to develop trained manpower in the health fields.

The Regents' Scholarship and Fellowship Programs provide both competitive and need-based scholarships for use at either public or private institutions of higher education within the state. The scholarships must be used for tuition and fees by full-time students and range in amount from $250 to $1,000 per year. In 1975–76 there were 73,387 awards, of which 43 percent (45 percent of the funds) went to private institutions. Total funds in 1975–76 for the program were $25.9 million but are decreasing—$23.8 million in 1976–77 and $10.6 million planned for 1977–78.

The largest program of student aid in New York is the Tuition Assistance Program. Grants, for use within the state, are based on need, and the maxima are $1,500 (the amount not to exceed cost of tuition) for undergraduates and $600 for graduate students. In 1975–76 the program was funded for $103.5 million, and 242,652 grants were made; 33 percent were used at private institutions, accounting for half of the funds. The program has been expanded, with funding up to $184.2 million in 1976–77 and over $200 million for 1977–78.

For students who are financially or educationally disadvantaged (or both) and are state residents, the Higher Education Opportunity Program provides funds to *institutions* attended by such students to assist in providing special educational opportunities. In 1975–76 the program served 5,300 students, with grants averaging $1,430. Funding in 1976–77 amounted to $7.6 million for students in private institutions in New York State.

A Guaranteed Loan Program allows students to borrow up to $7,500 to finance their education. In 1975–76, approximately 171,000 loans were made, totalling $233.5 million, and in 1976–77, slightly fewer loans (160,000) totalled $240 million.

Programs to serve medical and dental students and to increase health manpower pools include competitive scholarships for 400 students, ranging in amount from $350 to $1,000 per year, depending on need. Some of the scholarships (120) are reserved for students who will agree to serve, after they obtain degrees, in areas that have a shortage of medical personnel. In these cases, stipends are $1,000 for the first year of study and up to $4,000 for the next three years, depending on need.

In addition to medical and dental scholarships, New York provides capitation for nonpublic medical and dental schools amounting to $10.6 million in 1976–77 and $10.8 million for 1977–78. Grants are $1,500 for each lower-division and $2,500 for each upper-division student. Enrollment Expansion Aid to institutions provides $6,000 maximum for each additional upper-division medical student enrolled (over enrollments in a base year) and is designed to encourage enrollment of state residents returning from foreign medical schools to complete their educations. A Nursing Expansion Program has been phased out.

New York allows its scholarships and grants to be used at proprietary institutions as well as at private nonprofit institutions, but all must be used at institutions within the state (no portability).

Institutional grants. In addition to some programs mentioned above (such as the Higher Education Opportunity Program and medical/dental capitation grants) in which funds go directly to institutions but are closely tied to specific students and purposes, the so-called Bundy aid consists of grants to independent colleges and universities based on the number of degrees awarded. In 1976–77, funding amounted to $66.6 million, distributed as follows: $940 for each bachelor's degree awarded; $650 for each master's; $330 for each associate degree; and $3,100 for each doctorate.

New York State has endowed chairs in ten private institutions in the state in fields of science and the humanities, in the amount of $50,000 per chair per year. Other programs include that of the New York State Science and Technology Foundation, which in the past spent about $300,000 a year in research grants to public and private higher education institutions and other research organizations. Funding was cut in half in 1976–77, and no funds were appropriated for the programs in 1977–78. A special emergency grant to the Polytechnic Institute of New York in the amount of $500,000 in 1975–76 has not been renewed.

Pennsylvania

Constitutional provisions. The constitution of the Commonwealth of Pennsylvania allows some forms of assistance to private education institutions while prohibiting others. The "child benefit theory" has been accepted by the state courts in areas of health and safety, and released time programs for religious instruction not involving use of public buildings have been upheld. However, Article III, sec. 29 of the constitution prohibits appropriations "for charitable, educational or benevolent purposes to any person or community nor to any denomination or sectarian institution, corporation or association." Thus, direct appropriations to sectarian colleges are barred, although money may be directed to nonsectarian schools and colleges. Section 30 of the same article requires a two-thirds vote of the legislature to make such appropriations, but this has repeatedly occurred.

The constitution also specifically authorizes scholarship grants and loans to students at private as well as at public colleges and universities, and such programs need only fall within the area allowed by the First Amendment to the federal constitution in order to be valid.

Contracts. A contract program envisaged in the 1971 Master Plan has not yet been implemented, although there is a program for four private institutions to supply specific educational services (mainly home economics education), which is paid for by the state with money derived from federal vocational education programs. In 1976–77, that program was funded at $37,408.

Facilities. No state money goes toward construction or maintenance of private education facilities, but the state can provide consultation in order to help institutions obtain construction bonds at a low interest rate.

Student aid. The State Higher Education Grant Program makes awards up to $1,200 a year, on basis of need, for up to four years of education for Pennsylvania residents at institutions both within the state and outside it ($600 maximum on out-of-state grants). An award may not exceed one-third of the student's financial need or 80 percent of tuition and fees. Awards may be used at public or private higher education institutions and at hospitals, nursing schools, and private business and technical schools (proprietary institutions). In 1976–77, the program was funded at $68.4 million, of which about $39.5 million was used at private institutions of various kinds.

Senatorial scholarships, totalling about $8,000 in 1975-76, are awarded for use at four "state-related" institutions and at the private University of Pennsylvania. The state also funds a State-Wide College Work-Study Program and a Student Loan Guaranty Program.

Institutional Grants. Since 1974, Pennsylvania has provided direct aid, Institutional Assistance Grants, to eligible private institutions for each state scholarship recipient enrolled, in amounts up to $400 per student. These "trailer grants" were funded in 1976–77 at $12 million and carry the restriction that they cannot be used for sectarian or denominational expenses.

The state provides aid to private institutions in order to foster equal educational opportunity for disadvantaged students by funding remedial, tutorial, and counselling programs for such students. In 1976–77, this aid amounted to $3.4 million.

Pennsylvania also has an unusual program of direct aid to 13 private institutions, known as "state-aided" institutions. Aid is focused on specific programs within the institutions that are of benefit to the state, such as medical and health training. In 1976–77, the program was funded for about $36.7 million. The thirteen state-aided institutions are:

Delaware Valley College of Science and Agriculture
Dickinson School of Law
Drexel University
Hahnemann Medical College and Hospital of Philadelphia
Medical College of Pennsylvania (Women's Medical College)
Pennsylvania College of Optometry
Pennsylvania College of Podiatric Medicine
Pennsylvania College of Art
Philadelphia College of Osteopathic Medicine
Philadelphia College of the Performing Arts
Philadelphia College of Textiles and Science
Thomas Jefferson University
University of Pennsylvania

Coordination With Federal Programs

In making need-based awards, three of five states—California, New York, and Pennsylvania—require that the student make an application for a federally-funded Basic Educational Opportunity Grant, and any such grant is considered as a "resource" available to the student in calculating financial need and consequent state grants. Georgia has no requirement for a BEOG application as a condition for student aid, but both it and Illinois make their own calculations as to what a student might expect in the way of a BEOG, and they take that amount into consideration in making state awards.

Carnegie Council Survey of Private Universities and Four-Year Colleges in Selected States

One of the major purposes of our study of state policies toward private higher education was to determine, if possible, how programs of aid to private institutions affected their enrollment status, financial status, and institutional autonomy. However, in view of the wide variations among the states in amounts expended on aid to private higher education, it was apparent from the start that an important part of our attempt to assess the impact of state aid would have to be more explicitly focused on (1) a group of states with programs of aid to private higher education that were relatively substantial, and (2) a group of "control" states with relatively small expenditures on aid to private higher education. We also decided that this part of the study would have to be based on mailed question-naires addressed to private institutions of higher education, because data available in published form were seriously inadequate to provide the kinds of information we sought.

Accordingly, we selected six states (Group I) with compara-tively sizable programs of aid to private higher education—Cali-fornia, Illinois, Iowa, New York, Pennsylvania, and South Carolina—and eight states (Group II) with relatively small programs of aid—

Alabama, Florida, Kentucky, Massachusetts, Missouri, Tennessee, Virginia, and Washington. We also decided to limit the study to universities and four-year colleges, excluding private two-year institutions, which account for a relatively small proportion of total enrollment, and excluding, also, specialized institutions, which are not only a very heterogenous group but also tend to be located almost exclusively in large metropolitan areas and thus are largely non-existent in relatively less populous states.

From the universe of private universities and four-year colleges listed by the U.S. National Center for Education Statistics in the 14 states in 1974, we excluded those that did not have enrollment in both 1970 and 1974. This left 480 institutions, from which we drew a sample that was designed to be representative of five Carnegie categories: Research Universities, Other Doctoral-granting Universities, Comprehensive Universities and Colleges, Liberal Arts Colleges I, and Liberal Arts Colleges II. The initial sample selected in this manner included 299 institutions, of which 11 had closed or merged with another institution by May 1976, when our first group of questionnaires was mailed. Thus, we were left with a sample of 288 operating institutions.

Each institution was sent five questionnaires: (1) a questionnaire addressed to presidents, seeking information on their assessment of the economic position of their institutions and the impact of state aid; (2) a questionnaire addressed to vice-presidents of finance or similar administrators, seeking their views on the financial position of their institutions; (3) a questionnaire relating to financial statistics; (4) a questionnaire relating to financial aid to undergraduates; and (5) a questionnaire concerned with enrollment objectives, admissions data, and the impact of state student-aid programs.

The response rate was quite satisfactory, on the whole, although some institutions did not return all questionnaires, and some did not respond to all questions. Complete returns were received from 165 institutions and incomplete returns were received from 69; thus some information was available for 234 institutions, or 81 percent of the 288 institutions in operation in the spring of 1976. As Table 38 indicates, the percentage of nonrespondents tended to be somewhat smaller in Group I than in Group II states. Returns on

Table 38. Sample universe and rate of response, by Carnegie type of institution, Group I and Group II States

Type of institution	Institutions in sample		Institutions with complete response		Institutions with partial response		Institutions with non-response
	Number	Percent	Number	Percent	Number	Percent	Percent
Group I:							
Universities	15	9	8	8	4	11	20
Comprehensive universities and colleges	36	23	21	21	8	23	19
Highly selective liberal arts colleges	46	29	34	34	7	20	11
Other liberal arts colleges	52	39	37	37	16	46	15
Total:	159	100	100	100	35	100	15
Group II:							
Universities	10	8	4	6	4	12	20
Comprehensive universities and colleges	26	20	14	22	6	18	23
Highly selective liberal arts colleges	21	16	14	22	4	12	14
Other liberal arts colleges	72	56	33	51	20	59	26
Total:	129	100	65	100	34	100	23

Source: Carnegie Council survey.

some questionnaires were particularly small in universities in Group II states, of which, in any event, there are relatively few.

We shall find, however, that Liberal Arts Colleges II tend to form a considerably larger percentage of respondent institutions, on many of the items that will be analyzed, in Group II than in Group I states, while other types of institutions form a smaller percentage. This is not so much a result of differences in response rates as of differences in the relative representation of types of institutions in the original sample, which in turn reflected differences in the characteristics of private institutions in the two groups of states. In fact, Liberal Arts Colleges II formed 56 percent of the original sample in Group II states, compared with 39 percent in Group I states. This pronounced difference must always be kept in mind in interpreting differences on the various items we shall be examining between the two groups of states and underscores the importance of attaching more weight to differences between comparable groups of institutions than to differences between all respondent institutions in the two groups of states.

The differences in the characteristics of private institutions in the two groups of states, however, are significant from another perspective. The fact that relatively more of the institutions in Group I states were universities, comprehensive institutions, and relatively selective liberal arts colleges (the difference was especially pronounced for this group) suggests that there were more large, prestigious, and influential institutions in the Group I states that could affect legislative action in favor of private institutions.

Our analysis of the behavior of enrollment in Technical Supplement A indicates that there tend to be consistent differences between states with substantial programs of aid to private higher education and states with much more limited programs—the states with sizable programs of aid are likely to have had relatively large private sectors in 1963, and, as we have seen, a large private sector is particularly vulnerable, especially if it draws most of its students from within the state.

The Behavior of Enrollment

Before reviewing responses to questions relating to enrollment trends, we need to consider enrollment in Group I and Group II states and in our sample of institutions, as revealed by official enrollment statistics.

There was only a minor difference in the percentage increase in total enrollment in private universities and four-year colleges in the two groups of states from 1970 to 1975—7.3 percent in Group I states and 5.3 percent in Group II states (Table 39). On the whole, moreover, the pattern of differences among types of institutions was similar in the two groups of states. However, the increase in enrollment in both groups of liberal arts colleges was considerably greater in Group I than in Group II states.

Table 39. Enrollment in private universities and four-year colleges, by type, Group I and Group II States, 1970 and 1975 (numbers in thousands)

Group and type of institution	1970	1975	Percentage change
Group I states:	727.1	780.4	7.3
All universities	275.9	283.9	2.8
Research universities I	151.6	154.6	2.0
Research universities II	31.2	32.4	3.8
Other universities	93.1	97.2	4.4
Comprehensive universities and colleges	231.2	249.9	8.1
Liberal arts colleges I	79.2	87.4	10.4
Liberal arts colleges II	140.8	159.2	13.1
Group II states:	336.7	354.7	5.3
All universities	163.6	168.9	3.2
Research universities I	60.1	62.2	3.5
Research universities II	33.8	34.1	0.9
Other universities	69.7	72.6	4.2
Comprehensive universities and colleges	71.4	77.7	8.8
Liberal arts colleges I	27.2	27.7	1.8
Liberal arts colleges II	74.5	80.4	7.9

Source: Computed from data in Table 23.

Our respondent institutions experienced less pronounced growth in both groups of states than the universe of private institutions from which they were drawn (Table 40). This was particularly true of comprehensive universities and colleges in both groups of states and of Liberal Arts Colleges II in Group I states. On the other hand, our sample of Liberal Arts Colleges I in Group II states experienced a much larger increase in enrollment than its universe.

Full-time equivalent enrollment increased less rapidly than total enrollment in our sample Group I states, evidently reflecting the rising relative importance of part-time enrollment, especially in comprehensive universities and colleges and in Liberal Arts Colleges I.

Table 40. Percentage change in enrollment in private universities and four-year colleges, by type, total for all institutions, and total, full-time equivalent, and freshmen, respondent institutions, 1970 to 1975

Group and type of institution	Total	Respondent institutions[a]		
		Total	Full-time equivalent	Freshmen
Group I states:	7.3	4.6	2.8	−1.6
Universities	2.8	2.0	1.5	7.8
Comprehensive universities and colleges	8.1	5.4	1.8	−3.7
Liberal arts colleges I	10.4	11.6	6.7	−7.0
Liberal arts colleges II	13.1	6.1	5.3	−7.6
Group II states:	5.3	3.4	3.5	1.3
Universities	3.2	−0.6	0.1	0.9
Comprehensive universities and colleges	8.8	2.4	2.1	−3.3
Liberal arts colleges I	1.8	9.8	8.1	−1.1
Liberal arts colleges II	7.9	7.7	7.7	8.4

[a] Includes all respondent institutions that provided data on freshmen enrollment for both years.
Sources: Table 39 and Carnegie Council survey.

Differences in the behavior of total and FTE enrollment, on the other hand, were comparatively minor in Group II states, probably because there are fewer very large metropolitan areas with urban institutions attracting adult enrollment than in Group I states.

The behavior of freshman enrollment in our sample of institutions was notably more sluggish than that of either total or FTE enrollment, although there were exceptions in certain groups of institutions. This finding is yet another indication that, in a period of slowing growth of the college-age population, private colleges and universities, like their public counterparts, are becoming more dependent on part-time enrollment for survival.

Respondent institutions were asked to provide data on the number of full-time freshmen applicants and enrollment in 1970 and 1975, as well as on the proportions of full-time enrolled freshmen from within the state and from members of minority groups. The responses indicate that the number of applicants fell off much more than the number of enrolled freshmen in both groups of states and in most types of institutions (Table 41).

Ratios of applicants to enrollments tended to vary in the manner that would be expected, with the highest ratios prevailing among universities and Liberal Arts Colleges I in both groups of states. Furthermore, these ratios were surprisingly well maintained in most groups of institutions: though the decline in applicants was more pronounced than the decline in enrollments, the differences were not sufficiently pronounced to change the ratios greatly.

How do we explain the fact that a number of groups of institutions lost freshman enrollment despite the continuation of quite favorable ratios of applicants to enrollments? The answer probably lies in the fact that many would-be freshmen submit applicants to a number of institutions, so that an institution's ratios of applicants to enrollments may be deceptively high. The data suggest increased competition among institutions for a declining pool of applicants.

In attempting to assess the possible impact of differences in amounts of state aid to private institutions on enrollment in the two groups of states, more attention should be paid to complete enrollment data than to data for our sample of respondents, which has its deficiencies. Clearly, the most significant differences appear in the two liberal arts categories. When the behavior of enrollment in liberal arts colleges is examined more closely for individual states, however, it becomes clear that the more pronounced increase in enrollment in Liberal Arts Colleges I in Group I states is largely explained by spectacular increases in a relatively small number of institutions in New York State, and these increases in turn were largely in part-time enrollment. In Liberal Arts Colleges II, the larger gains in Group I states were explained by substantial increases in New York and California: in New York some of the pronounced gains were in colleges with large proportions of part-time enrollment, while in California there were a number of newly listed institutions in the Liberal Arts II category (see discussion of newly listed institutions in Technical Supplement A). State student-aid programs may have

Table 41. Freshman applicants and enrollments, Group I and Group II States, Carnegie Council sample survey, 1970 and 1975

Group and type of institutions	Number of respondents	Applicants			Enrollments			Ratio of applicants to enrollments	
		1970	1975	Percentage change	1970	1975	Percentage change	1970	1975
Group I states:	100	160,813	153,303	−4.7	50,898	50,086	−1.6	3.2	3.1
Universities	13	56,383	59,754	+6.0	15,578	16,794	+7.8	3.6	3.6
Comprehensive universities and colleges	21	51,797	47,185	−8.9	15,401	14,832	−3.7	3.4	3.2
Liberal arts colleges I	33	33,796	30,252	−10.5	10,469	9,732	−7.0	3.2	3.1
Liberal arts colleges II	33	18,837	16,112	−14.5	9,450	8,728	−7.6	2.0	1.8
Group II states:	65	92,043	80,786	−12.2	26,440	26,786	+1.3	3.5	3.0
Universities	6	35,819	26,729	−25.4	7,169	7,235	+0.9	5.0	3.7
Comprehensive universities and colleges	15	21,406	20,419	−4.6	7,470	7,222	−3.3	2.9	2.8
Liberal arts colleges I	14	19,649	18,364	−6.5	4,883	4,831	−1.1	4.0	3.8
Liberal arts colleges II	30	15,169	15,274	+0.7	6,918	7,498	+8.4	2.2	2.0

Source: Carnegie Council survey.

played a role in stimulating some of these gains—awards are permitted for part-time students in California and in New York's tuition assistance program, while new listings, as we suggested in Technical Supplement A, may well be stimulated by both federal and state aid.

On the other hand, gains in the liberal arts categories were minor or negative in Illinois, Iowa, and Pennsylvania among Group I states and quite substantial in Liberal Arts Colleges II in Florida and Massachusetts among Group II states. Iowa and Pennsylvania both had overall enrollment growth rates that were well below average from 1970 to 1975, while Florida's rate of growth was well above average, and that of Massachusetts was only slightly below the national rate of growth of total enrollment (5.4 percent—see Table 23). Thus, as we recognized at the start, differences in the behavior of enrollment among the states are influenced by many factors, of which the existence of a substantial program of federal aid to private higher education is only one.

When the presidents of responding institutions were asked how their institutions' positions had changed, compared with five years ago, with respect to their ability to attract and hold the desired number of students, slightly more than three-fifths of the presidents in Group II states, compared with slightly more than one-half of those in Group I states, said that the position had improved. Similar differences prevailed for the various types of institutions, except in the case of Liberal Arts Colleges II, where improvement was indicated by a slightly larger percentage of presidents in Group I than in Group II.

All in all, we are inclined to believe that the analysis in Technical Supplement A, which showed that there was a slight tendency toward a negative relationship between amounts spent on aid to private higher education per FTE and ability of the state's private institutions to hold their share of enrollment (Table 33), is more conclusive than anything we can say about Group I and Group II states. We repeat—losses in states with large private sectors might have been considerably greater in the absence of state aid programs.

Returning to questionnaire responses, the percentage of minority group freshmen tended to be somewhat higher in Group I than in Group II states and to increase somewhat between 1970 and 1975, but the differences were small (Table 42).

Table 42. Members of minority groups and state residents as percentages of
enrolled freshmen, by type of institution, Group I and Group II States,
Carnegie Council sample survey, 1970 and 1975

Group and type of institution	Members of minority groups[a]			State residents		
	1970	1975	Change in percentage points	1970	1975	Change in percentage points
Group I states:	6.9	9.0	+2.1	63.4	64.1	+0.7
Universities	9.8	11.4	+1.6	61.4	63.2	+1.8
Comprehensive universities and colleges	6.0	7.8	+1.8	70.5	65.3	−5.2
Liberal arts colleges I	6.4	7.3	+0.9	55.2	57.4	+2.2
Liberal arts colleges II	5.4	9.7	+7.6	63.6	70.4	+6.8
Group II states:	5.7	7.2	+1.5	37.9	40.8	+2.9
Universities	6.8	7.6	+0.8	27.1	32.5	+5.4
Comprehensive universities and colleges	5.4	7.7	+2.3	44.2	44.5	+0.3
Liberal arts colleges I	6.7	7.2	+0.5	30.8	31.7	+0.9
Liberal arts colleges II	3.8	6.2	+2.4	47.2	51.1	+3.9

[a] Predominantly black colleges are omitted from these computations.

Source: Carnegie Council survey.

Far more significant were the differences in proportions of
freshmen who were state residents. These percentages tended to be
considerably higher in Group I than in Group II states in all
categories of institutions. On the whole, the differences were
consistent with those indicated by 1972 NCES data for all of the states
(See Table 22).

Also of considerable interest was the fact that, although the
percentages of freshmen who were state residents rose somewhat
between 1970 and 1975 in both groups of states and in most categories
of institutions, the increases were quite small. Surprisingly, also,
increases tended to be smaller in Group I than in Group II states
(except in Liberal Arts II Colleges), even though most Group I states
did not permit awards to students planning to enroll outside the
state.

Clearly, private institutions that draw most of their students
from within their states have more to gain from student-aid programs
than institutions that attract large proportions of students from other
states, given the general reluctance of state legislatures to grant

student aid to residents of other states or to students attending college in other states. Thus, the larger proportions of state residents among Group I freshmen help to explain the more generous programs of aid to private higher education in those states. It is perhaps somewhat surprising that the proportion of state residents among their freshmen increased so little between 1970 and 1975.

Patterns of Student Aid

Perhaps the most fruitful part of our sample survey related to student aid. The fact that both federal and state funds for student aid were increasing sharply over the period covered by our data, 1970–71 to 1975–76, is well known (Table 43). By definition, also, amounts provided for state undergraduate aid were far smaller in Group II than in Group I states.

Current-fund revenues for student aid increased relatively slowly in both groups of states. These funds include federal Supplementary Educational Opportunity Grants (SEOG), federal direct student loans, state student-aid funds allocated directly to institutions (an infrequent item), and private gifts and endowment income restricted to student aid. Respondents were instructed not to include federal work-study funds in current-fund revenues, even though these funds are allocated to institutions, along with SEOG and direct student loan funds. Thus, we show work-study funds as a separate item.

The relatively slow growth of current-fund revenues for student-aid reflects the comparatively small increases in SEOG and direct student loan appropriations and the generally modest increases in gift and endowment funds allocated for student aid over the period. Differences among particular groups of institutions must be interpreted with caution where the number of respondents is small, as in the case of universities in Group II states.[1]

Federal Basic Educational Opportunity Grant (BEOG) funds were, of course, nonexistent in 1970–71—the program was adopted by Congress in 1972 and first became operative in 1972–73—but were quite substantial in both Group I and Group II states by 1975–76.

---

[1] The number of institutions included in Table 43 varies from item to item within each category, but the number of respondents for each item is the same in 1970–71 and 1975–76.

Table 43. Student-aid funds, respondent private institutions, by type, and source of funds, Group I and Group II States, 1970-71 and 1975-76 (amounts in thousands of dollars)

Type of institution and source of funds[a]	Group I States				Group II States			
	Number of respondents	1970-71	1975-76	Percentage change	Number of respondents	1970-71	1975-76	Percentage change
Universities								
Current fund revenues for student aid[b]	10	35,999	40,521	13	4	12,583	10,801	−14
Federal BEOG	10		4,330		5		1,427	
Federal work-study	9	965	2,105	118	5	1,153	2,042	77
State undergraduate aid received directly by students	9	12,010	23,792	98	5	320	1,717	44
Total from above sources	7	28,776	43,183	50	5	14,226	16,268	14
Student aid deficit[c]	10	23,217	33,125	43	5	9,457	16,201	71
Comprehensive universities and colleges								
Current fund revenues for student aid[b]	21	7,747	11,922	54	11	2,857	4,581	60
Federal BEOG	22		6,510		17		3,197	
Federal work-study	18	1,132	2,218	84	17	1,215	2,728	125
State undergraduate aid received directly by students	20	13,582	25,505	88	14	177	1,055	496
Total from above sources	16	18,604	34,843	87	11	3,609	9,137	153
Student aid deficit[c]	21	12,246	20,289	66	13	2,888	3,769	30
Selective liberal arts colleges								
Current fund revenues for student aid[b]	29	7,380	9,186	24	11	2,945	3,700	26
Federal BEOG	35	652	3,456		14		1,363	
Federal work-study	30		1,552	138	14	843	1,495	77
State undergraduate aid received directly by students	30	7,105	12,607	77	10	168	439	161
Total from above sources	26	14,174	24,011	69	9	4,836	7,972	65
Student aid deficit[c]	31	6,623	9,220	39	13	2,058	2,681	30

Other liberal arts colleges

Current fund revenues for student aid[b]	32	4,101	5,385	31	28	2,586	4,593	78
Federal BEOG	42		8,181		39		7,448	
Federal work-study	36	1,878	3,741	99	35	2,471	4,090	66
State undergraduate aid received directly by students	34	5,353	13,851	159	32	105	1,249	1,089
Total from above sources	28	9,691	25,335	161	27	4,517	13,722	204
Student aid deficit[c]	33	4,881	6,306	29	34	2,901	5,109	76

All respondent institutions

Current fund revenues for student aid[b]	92	55,227	67,014	21	54	20,971	23,675	13
Federal BEOG	103		22,447		75		13,435	
Federal work-study	93	4,703	9,616	104	71	5,682	10,355	82
State undergraduate aid received directly by students	93	38,050	75,755	99	61	770	4,460	479
Total from above sources	77	71,245	127,372	79	52	27,188	47,099	73
Student aid deficit[c]	95	46,967	68,948	47	65	17,304	27,760	60

[a] Does not include student loans, social security benefits, veterans' benefits, state work-study funds, or minor state programs for veterans, orphans, etc.

[b] Includes federal SEOG funds but does not include federal work-study or loan funds. Federal BEOG funds were reported separately.

[c] Student-aid deficit equals total student-aid expenditures by the institution less total current-fund revenues for student aid.

Source: Carnegie Council survey.

Amounts available for federal work-study awards also increased
sharply, as did state undergraduate aid received directly by students.
The far higher percentage increase in state undergraduate aid funds
in Group II states reflects, of course, the fact that funds from this
source were very small in these states in 1970–71. They continued to
be far smaller than in Group I states in 1975–76.

Nevertheless, the percentage increase in total funds from all of
these sources was strikingly similar in the two groups of states (79
percent in Group I states and 73 percent in Group II states). Even so—
and this is a particularly significant finding—student-aid deficits
increased very substantially over the perod in both Group I and
Group II states and in all individual categories of institutions.

How do we account for the substantial increase in student-aid
deficits (the excess of institutional funds expended for student aid
over funds received by the institution for student aid) in a period
when federal and state allocations for student aid were increasing
sharply?

So far as we can determine, there were three reasons for this
rather surprising development. The period was characterized, of
course, by a high rate of inflation and by pronounced tution increases
necessitated by rising costs. Whenever institutions raise their tuition,
they tend to try to increase amounts allocated for student aid in order
not to increase educational costs for needy students. Secondly, during
these years, many private institutions were striving to increase the
diversity of their student bodies by recruiting more widely, especially
among lower-income and minority groups. Successful recruiting for
students in these groups is often contingent on an increase in funds
available for student aid. And in the third place—probably at least
partly explained by the recruiting of disadvantaged students—the
percentages of undergraduates receiving some type of student aid
increased considerably over the period, as we shall see at a later point.

Thus far, we have not adjusted for differences in institutional
enrollment, which were larger overall in Group I than in Group II
states and, of course, enrollment tended to be larger in universities
than in other groups of institutions. Table 44 presents the same data
on student aid on a per full-time equivalent (FTE) student basis.
Percentage changes in amounts available for student aid on this basis
differed relatively little from changes shown in Table 43, reflecting

the fact that FTE enrollment changes were not large. However, total amounts available per FTE were larger in Group I than in Group II states, reflecting the larger amounts per FTE for state undergraduate student aid. And yet the student aid deficit per FTE was slightly larger in Group I than in Group II states, as was total funded and unfunded aid per FTE.

The pronounced increase in the proportion of undergraduates receiving some form of financial aid is indicated in Panel B of Table 45. Overall, the proportion rose from about 47 to 59 percent in Group I states and from about 40 to 54 percent in Group II states. Moreover, increases showed up in all categories of institutions, but with a fairly consistent pattern of somewhat smaller percentages of undergraduates receiving aid in Group II than in Group I states.

When we look at Panel C, however, we find that the percentages of grants, scholarships, and tuition waivers, while increasing in both groups of institutions over the period, were considerably higher in Group I than in Group II states—in all categories of institutions. Undoubtedly, this consistent difference reflected the more substantial programs of state student aid in Group I states.

As for percentages of undergraduates receiving aid from the institution's own budget—Panel A—differences between Group I and Group II states were very small. This is not particularly surprising in view of the fact that state student-aid funds do not usually flow through institutional budgets but are typically awarded directly to students.

Now let us look more closely at the fact that the difference between the percentage of undergraduates receiving *some form of aid* in Group I and Group II states was considerably smaller than the difference in the percentage receiving grant aid. This finding suggests that students in Group II states were relatively more dependent on loans and work-study funds than were students in Group I states. When we investigated this matter more directly, we found that percentages of students receiving loans of some sort were not greatly different in the two groups of states, although the percentage increased somewhat more in Group II than in Group I over the period. All in all, the percentage of undergraduates who received loans increased from about 25 to 28 percent in Group I states and from 20 to 26 percent in Group II states between 1970-71 and 1975-76.

Table 44. Student-aid funds per full-time equivalent student, Group I and Group II States, 1970-71 and 1975-76

Type of institution and source of funds[a]	Group I States			Group II States		
	1970-71	1975-76	Percentage change	1970-71	1975-76	Percentage change
Universities						
Current fund revenues for student aid[b]	352	456	29	287	252	-12
Federal BEOG	–	44	–	–	32	–
Federal work-study	14	31	121	26	46	77
State undergraduate	149	228	54	7	39	457
Total from above sources	515	759	47	320	369	15
Student aid deficit[c]	218	353	62	213	369	73
Total funded and unfunded aid	733	1,112	52	533	739	39
Comprehensive universities and colleges						
Current fund revenues for student aid[b]	97	146	50	113	176	56
Federal BEOG	–	68	–	–	86	–
Federal work-study	19	31	63	25	63	152
State undergraduate	180	298	66	7	33	371
Total from above sources	296	543	83	145	358	147
Student aid deficit[c]	148	220	49	104	127	22
Total funded and unfunded aid	443	763	72	250	484	94
Selective liberal arts colleges						
Current fund revenues for student aid[b]	230	267	16.1	326	420	29
Federal BEOG	–	87	–	–	88	–
Federal work-study	20	46	130	51	90	76
State undergraduate	208	349	68	14	33	136
Total from above sources	458	749	64	391	631	61
Student aid deficit[c]	173	248	43	117	124	6.0
Total funded and unfunded aid	631	997	58	508	755	49

Other liberal arts colleges

Current fund revenues for student aid[b]	176	131	13	117	188	61
Federal BEOG	46	163	70	91	207	52
Federal work-study	152	78	123.0	5	138	840
State undergraduate		339			47	
Total from above sources	314	711	126	213	580	172
Student aid deficit[c]	137	201	47	92	176	91
Total funded and unfunded aid	450	913	103	306	756	147
All respondent institutions						
Current fund revenues for student aid[b]	202	257	27	215	240	12
Federal BEOG	22	82	91	42	91	81
Federal work-study	170	42	73	8	76	388
State undergraduate		294			39	
Total from above sources	394	675	70	265	446	68
Student aid deficit	172	261	52	150	238	59
Total funded and unfunded aid	556	936	65	415	683	65

[a] Does not include student loans, social security benefits, veterans' benefits, state work-study funds, or minor state programs for veterans, etc.

[b] Includes federal SEOG funds but does not include federal work-study or loan funds. Federal BEOG funds were reported separately.

[c] Student-aid deficit equals total student-aid expenditures by the institution less total current-fund revenues for student aid.

Source: Carnegie Council survey.

Table 45. Undergraduates who received student aid, Group I and Group II States, 1970-71 and 1975-76

	Group I States			Group II States		
Type of institution	Number of institutions	1970-71	1975-76	Number of institutions	1970-71	1975-76
Panel A: Percentage of undergraduate students who received some form of financial aid from institution's budget						
Universities	7	27.3	33.2	3	25.2	28.8
Comprehensive universities and colleges	12	16.9	26.4	13	19.8	29.5
Selective liberal arts colleges	22	36.2	40.3	13	36.7	40.0
Other liberal arts colleges	27	32.2	39.8	23	33.3	40.5
All respondents	68	26.2	33.6	52	27.8	34.7
Panel B: Percentage of undergraduate students receiving some form of financial aid[a]						
Universities	6	44.9	54.1	4	33.8	45.8
Comprehensive universities and colleges	9	42.2	59.9	12	34.2	53.1
Selective liberal arts colleges	20	47.7	55.5	13	40.2	45.7
Other liberal arts colleges	26	56.0	65.9	28	48.5	64.2
All respondents	61	47.0	58.7	57	39.6	53.7
Panel C: Percentage of undergraduate students who received grants, scholarships or tuition waivers						
Universities	3	42.1	50.8	3	26.8	30.1
Comprehensive universities and colleges	11	38.0	49.1	10	17.0	32.1
Selective liberal arts colleges	20	39.0	44.1	12	35.0	39.3
Other liberal arts colleges	20	43.2	57.2	24	31.8	46.6
All respondents	54	40.0	50.0	49	27.2	38.0

[a] This represents an unduplicated count of students who received financial aid in any form.

Source: Carnegie Council survey.

However, many students, of course, receive both grants and loans. And, not surprisingly, the percentage of undergraduates receiving *only* loans or work-study funds was in fact higher in Group II than in Group I states. In Group I states, the percentage receiving only loans or work-study funds rose from 7 to 8 percent over the period, while in Group II states it rose from 12 to 15 percent.

Not only were students in Group I states more likely to receive grant aid than those in Group II states, but relatively fewer of the recipients of aid in Group I states were from low-income families than was the case in Group II states. This information, sought only for the year 1974–75, showed that in Group I states an estimated 26 percent of the students who received some form of aid came from families with an annual gross income of less than $9,000, compared with 38 percent in Group II states. On the other hand, in Group I states an estimated 19 percent of the students who received aid came from families with incomes of $18,000 and over, compared with an estimated 13 percent in Group II states.

A closer look at the data, however, indicates that state scholarship policies probably explain only a minor part of this difference. Consider first the fact that universities and Liberal Arts Colleges I tended to aid relatively more students in the $18,000 or more family income bracket than other groups of institutions. This is not surprising, because it is these institutions that are especially concerned with student ability and that also are more likely to have endowment income available for student aid. They may well tend to use some of their institutional funds to attract able students from upper middle income families that would not qualify for either federal or state student grants. Moreover, a considerably larger proportion of respondent institutions were from these categories in Group I (44 percent) than in Group II states (19 percent).

Secondly, five of the eight Group II states, but only one of the six Group I states, were in the South. Southern states tend to have low per capita incomes and thus relatively more students in low-income brackets than states outside the South—though the effect of low per capita income, is, of course, at least partly offset by low enrollment rates of students from low-income families. However, the data in Table 46 indicate that the percentages of undergraduate recipients from families with incomes under $9,000 were comparatively high in all of

Table 46. Percentage distribution of undergraduates receiving any form of student aid, by family gross income, Group I and Group II States, by type of institution and state, 1974-75

Group, type of institution, and state	Number of respondents	Less than $9,000	$9,000 to 11,999	$12,000 to 14,999	$15,000 to 17,999	$18,000 and over	Total
Group I:							
Universities	68	25.8	19.0	19.9	16.6	18.7	100.0
	7	24.8	15.7	17.8	16.9	24.8	100.0
Comprehensive universities							
and colleges	13	24.2	25.2	22.0	17.0	11.6	100.0
Liberal arts I colleges	23	25.0	15.3	19.6	16.3	23.8	100.0
Liberal arts II colleges	25	33.3	17.1	19.6	15.0	15.0	100.0
Group II:							
Universities	47	37.6	20.7	17.6	10.9	13.2	100.0
	1	30.0	16.2	14.4	23.8	15.6	100.0
Comprehensive universities							
and colleges	10	29.6	23.1	20.6	13.6	13.1	100.0
Liberal arts I colleges	8	37.6	15.4	14.4	9.8	22.8	100.0
Liberal arts II colleges	28	49.3	19.3	15.3	7.6	8.5	100.0
Group I:							
California	68	25.8	19.0	19.9	16.6	18.7	100.0
Illinois	12	24.1	16.0	18.8	19.6	21.5	100.0
Iowa	11	23.2	23.8	19.2	15.9	17.9	100.0
New York	7	31.3	20.3	20.0	12.6	15.8	100.0
Pennsylvania	15	26.0	15.1	17.6	16.9	24.4	100.0
South Carolina	17	24.0	20.5	24.5	17.1	13.9	100.0
	6	48.6	10.0	14.3	13.2	13.9	100.0

Group II:	47	37.6	20.7	17.6	10.9	13.2	100.0
Alabama	3	53.7	22.4	12.0	6.6	5.3	100.0
Florida	7	58.8	20.8	14.1	3.9	2.4	100.0
Kentucky	5	61.6	17.4	16.1	3.7	1.2	100.0
Massachusetts	10	24.5	19.9	20.3	14.3	21.0	100.0
Missouri	4	20.3	22.4	18.4	10.7	28.2	100.0
Tennessee	7	44.2	18.0	14.8	12.3	10.7	100.0
Virginia	8	41.3	21.1	17.3	11.8	8.5	100.0
Washington	5	29.3	18.3	18.5	11.4	22.5	100.0
South (without black colleges)	25	39.3	19.5	17.3	12.6	11.3	100.0
Non-South	81	24.8	19.5	20.0	16.3	19.4	100.0

Source: Carnegie Council survey.

the Southern states. This finding is partly attributable to the presence of a few black colleges, with their typically low-income students, among the respondent institutions. But even when the black colleges are eliminated, the percentage of recipients from families with incomes under $9,000 was 39.3 percent in the Southern states and 24.8 percent in the states outside the South.

Nevertheless, we cannot altogether rule out the influence of state scholarship programs in enabling more young people from middle and upper-middle income families to obtain student aid. In their analysis of federal student-aid programs, Atelsek and Gomberg (1975, p. 18) showed that about 29 percent of dependent undergraduates receiving aid under the State Student Incentive Grant program in 1974-75 were from families with incomes of $12,000 or more (their highest income category), compared with only 8.5 percent in the BEOG program and 6.5 percent in the SEOG program. Moreover, some of the state scholarship and grant programs aiding students in private institutions, as we have seen (Table 17), take account of ability as well as need (a policy that is likely to raise the income distribution of aided students somewhat within the income group eligible for aid, because of the high correlation between family income and test scores). In addition, most states use family contribution schedules that are somewhat less restrictive than the schedule used in the federal BEOG program. Here is the tally on criteria for aid and the family contribution schedule used in our six Group I states (using data for the largest program aiding students in private higher education from Table 17 and Boyd, 1977, p. 17).

State	Criteria for aid	Family contribution schedule
California	Ability and need	College Scholarship Service
Illinois	Need	State's own schedule
Iowa	Need	College Scholarship Service
New York	Need	State's own schedule
Pennsylvania	Need	State's own schedule
South Carolina	Ability and need	College Scholarship Service and state's own schedule

Our data hint at another possible indirect effect of state scholarship programs—universities and Liberal Arts Colleges I tend to aid relatively more students from families with incomes of $18,000 or more than do either comprehensive universities and colleges or Liberal Arts Colleges II. To the extent that students receive grants from either federal or state sources, institutional funds available for student aid are released as supplements to these sources and may well be used, as least in part, to attract able students from families with income somewhat above the maxima applicable to either federal or state programs. This effect would clearly be more significant in states with sizable student-aid programs than in states with very limited state programs. And, as suggested earlier, universities and Liberal Arts Colleges I tend to have relatively more endowment income that may be used for this purpose.

The Financial Condition of Institutions

Thus far, we have found no evidence that private institutions in Group I states were able to maintain or increase enrollments more effectively than those in Group II states, although they were able to provide more grant aid for students and to aid relatively more students from middle and upper-middle income families. What about the impact of state aid programs on the financial status of institutions?

A number of studies conducted around 1970, when there was grave concern about the financial crisis in higher education, indicated that a sizable proportion of private institutions were incurring operating deficits. Several studies also provided evidence that student-aid deficits were a major factor in giving rise to these operating deficits.[2]

We obtained data on operating surpluses and deficits for each year from 1970–71 to 1976–77, although not all of our respondents were able to provide data for all of these years. For the most part, we shall report these data per FTE, because the significance of a surplus

---

[2] See, for example, Cheit (1971); Jellema (1971); Jenny and Wynn (1970); and Association of Independent Collges and Universities of Ohio (1971).

or deficit of a given magnitude relates to the size of the institution.

Our data indicate that the financial status of respondent institutions tended to improve, on the whole, from 1970–71—a year of deficits, as expected—to 1973–74, but that after that the situation deteriorated (Table 47)[3]. It is important, however, to bear in mind that data for 1976–77, and to some extent data for 1975–76, are based on estimates. Although trends for the two groups of institutions were similar, the overall balance per FTE tended to be more favorable in Group II than in Group I states throughout the period. This trend was not true, however, for individual groups of institutions, though the number of respondents, especially of universities in Group II states, is too small in some cases to provide reliable data. But there was some tendency for liberal arts colleges in Group II states to have larger deficits in years after 1973–74 than in Group I states, and there was also a tendency in both groups of states for liberal arts colleges to have relatively large and persistent deficits per FTE (though an appreciable estimated decline occurred in Liberal Arts Colleges II in Group II states between 1975–76 and 1976–77).

The serious impact of a high inflation rate on the budgetary positions of institutions of higher education is by now a familiar phenomenon and was identified by Harris (1970) in his history of Havard's economic status as a problem for Harvard in every period of serious inflation. In the bottom line of Table 47, we show the percentage increase in the Consumer Price Index of the Bureau of Labor Statistics for the year *preceding* each academic year in the table, on the ground that it is the inflation rate in the preceding year that influences the rate of increase of faculty and other salaries and other important budgetary items (such as supplies purchased at the beginning of an academic year). The data suggest that the improvement in the operating balances of our respondent institutions was assisted by comparatively low inflation rates, especially in 1971–72 and 1972–73 (the period, it will be recalled, when price controls were in effect). Undoubtedly, the deterioration in operating balances after 1972–73 was related to, if not entirely caused by, accelerated inflation in 1973–74 and 1974–75 (resulting in part from oil price increases,

[3] Table 47 includes only those institutions that provided data on surpluses and deficits for each year.

Table 47. Operating surplus or deficit per full-time equivalent student, Group I and Group II States, 1970-71 to 1976-77

State	Number of institutions	1970-71	1971-72	1972-73	1973-74	1974-75	1975-76	1976-77
Universities								
Group I	10	−109	91	−87	12	−57	28	−165
Group II	4	−81	113	215	342	393	97	122
Comprehensive universities and colleges								
Group I	18	−10	16	−1	44	12	20	4
Group II	15	0	73	47	−10	4	8	6
Selective liberal arts colleges								
Group I	29	−89	9	64	95	−48	−82	−71
Group II	13	69	−37	−43	−117	−90	−142	−139
Other liberal arts colleges								
Group I	32	−50	10	−10	24	−26	−41	−56
Group II	30	−60	17	42	−5	−102	−87	−32
All respondent institutions								
Group I	89	−68	45	−28	36	−30	2	−86
Group II	62	−31	60	91	95	99	−4	16
Percentage increase in Consumer Price Index (preceding year)		5.7	5.0	3.8	4.8	8.4	10.3	7.6

Note: Includes only those institutions that provided data on surpluses and deficits for each year.

Source: Carnegie Council survey (numbers for 1975-76 and 1976-77 are based on estimates).

which created particularly difficult problems for colleges and universities in states with severe winters).

As we proceed with our analysis, however, we shall find that deterioration in operating balances was also strongly influenced by other problems, such as declining enrollment.

In Table 48, we have summarized the operating positions of all the institutions and classified each year's outcome as surplus, deficit, or zero balance. For Group I states, more institutions had a deficit in 1970–71 than in any other year. However, roughly one-third of the institutions in those states continued to have a deficit position in each year thereafter. In Group II states, slightly more institutions had deficits in 1973–74 and 1974–75 than in 1970–71, but the number with deficits declined somewhat in the following two years.

Table 48. Number of institutions with operating surplus or deficit, Group I and Group II States, 1970-71 to 1976-77

| | In Group I States | | | In Group II States | | |
Year	Surplus	Deficit	Zero balance	Surplus	Deficit	Zero balance
1970-71	35	50	4	34	28	0
1971-72	50	34	5	37	24	1
1972-73	52	32	5	41	20	1
1973-74	57	27	5	30	31	1
1974-75	46	38	5	31	29	2
1975-76	50	30	9	31	22	9
1976-77	44	28	17	34	14	14

Source: Carnegie Council survey (numbers for 1975-76 and 1976-77 are based on estimates).

A more detailed analysis of the data (not shown) indicates that percentages with deficits were particularly high in 1975–76 among Liberal Arts Colleges I in Group I states and among Liberal Arts Colleges II in Group II states. However, when we consider the percentages with declines in operating balances from 1973–74 to 1975–76, it was the Liberal Arts College I in both groups of states that were particularly likely to experience declines.

We have earlier noted that student-aid deficits increased appreciably from 1970–71 to 1975–76 in both total and per FTE terms. Table 49, which compares average student-aid deficits per FTE with

Table 49. Student-aid deficit and operating surplus or deficit per full-time equivalent student, Group I and Group II States, 1970-71 and 1975-76

	Group I States						Group II States					
	Number of institutions in sample[a]		1970-71		1975-76		Number of institutions in sample[a]		1970-71		1975-76	
			Student-aid deficit	Operating surplus or deficit (−)	Student-aid deficit	Operating surplus or deficit (−)			Student-aid deficit	Operating surplus or deficit (−)	Student-aid deficit	Operating surplus or deficit (−)
Universities	10	10	−$218	−$109	−$311	$28	5	5	−$213	−$77	−$369	$81
Comprehensive universities and colleges	21	18	−145	−10	−239	20	13	15	−88	0	−113	8
Liberal arts colleges I	31	31	−175	88	−232	−83	13	13	−122	69	−155	−141
Liberal arts colleges II	33	34	−139	−46	−200	−38	33	33	−99	−65	−168	−92
All respondent institutions	95	93	−178	−67	−260	1	65	66	−140	−32	−221	−9

[a] First column is student-aid deficit and second is operating surplus or deficit.

Source: Carnegie Council survey.

operating surpluses or deficits per FTE in both of those years, indicates that student-aid deficits were more unfavorable in both years than operating balances. In both groups of states, the operating balance (for all reporting institutions) compared more favorably with the student-aid deficit in 1975-76 than in 1970-71. This situation is not true, however, for Liberal Arts Colleges I in either Group I or Group II states. Moreover, these colleges had not, on the average, had operating deficits in 1970-71 but did have them in 1975-76.

In an attempt to identify the institutions in relative financial difficulty in the last three years or so, we have used a combination of criteria:

1. The institution had an operating deficit that averaged $100 or more per FTE student a year during the years from 1974-75 to 1976-77.
2. The institution's debt service per FTE in 1976-77 was well above the average for its type of institution.
3. The institution's endowment fund balance per FTE in 1974-75 (the most recent year reported) was well below the average for its type of institution.
4. The institution's enrollment tended to be declining.
5. The chief financial officer characterized the institution's financial condition as "somewhat unfavorable" or in "serious distress."

Classification of the institution as in a weak position depended on a *combination* of several of these signs of weaknesses—one sign of weakness alone did not suffice. Moreover, several institutions that were running operating deficits and showing other signs of current financial weakness but nevertheless had relatively high endowment fund balances per FTE were classified as in a "middle" rather than in a weak position because they were not considered to be in jeopardy.

Institutions that we classified as strong met the following criteria:

1. Their operating balances tended to be positive or zero.
2. Their debt service tended to be relatively low.
3. Their enrollments were relatively stable or rising.

4. Their endowment fund balances per FTE were relatively high, or at least about average, for their type of institution.

5. The chief financial officer characterized the institution's position as "holding steady," "somewhat favorable," or "good to excellent."

In addition, following the practice of the Bowen-Minter reports, we have classified the institution's position as "gaining ground," "holding steady," or "losing ground." This classification also depended on a combination of financial criteria, including changes in fund balances and the trend in enrollment.

The results are indicated in Table 50. They show that they great majority of institutions in both Group I and Group II states were in a "middle position"; 16 percent of Group I institutions and 21 percent of Group II institutions were considered to be in a "weak position"; and 5 percent in Group I and 7 percent in Group II in a strong position.

Nearly all of the institutions classified as weak were in either Liberal Arts I or Liberal Arts II categories, especially the latter, and since Liberal Arts Colleges II were relatively more numerous among Group II respondents, perhaps the most significant comparison relates to this relatively vulnerable category of institutions. We find that 35 percent of Liberal Arts Colleges II in Group II were in weak condition, compared with 22 percent in Group I. This is perhaps the clearest indication that we have found as yet that state aid policies in Group I states may be assisting private colleges in maintaining their financial stability.

Relatively more institutions were gaining ground in Group I than in Group II states, but slightly more were losing ground. The latter difference, however, cannot be considered particularly significant.

How do our results compare with those of Bowen and Minter? Close agreement cannot be expected, because of differences in the characteristics of the samples and in the measures used. Moreover, we had estimates of operating balances for 1976–77, while the most recent year for which Bowen and Minter had data on these balances was 1975–76.

Even so, the results are not very different, comparing the data in Table 50 with the corresponding data in their most recent

Table 50. Number of institutions, by estimated current financial condition and recent trend in condition, Group I and Group II States, by type of institution, 1976-77 (items in parentheses are percents)

Group, type of institution, and current condition	Recent trend in condition			
	Gaining ground	Holding steady	Losing ground	Total
Group I:	6 (6)	65 (65)	29 (29)	100 (100)
Strong		5		5 (5)
Middle	5	58	16	79 (79)
Weak	1	2	13	16 (16)
Universities	1	8	2	11 (100)
Strong		1		1 (9)
Middle		7	2	9 (82)
Weak	1			1 (9)
Comprehensive universities and colleges	1	16	5	22 (100)
Strong		2		2 (9)
Middle	1	14	4	19 (87)
Weak			1	1 (4)
Liberal arts colleges I	2	19	10	31 (100)
Strong		2		2 (6)
Middle	2	16	5	23 (75)
Weak		1	5	6 (19)
Liberal arts colleges II	2	22	12	36 (100)
Strong				0 (0)
Middle	2	21	5	28 (78)
Weak		1	7	8 (22)
Group II:	(0)	53 (75)	18 (25)	71 (100)
Strong		5		5 (7)
Middle		45	6	51 (72)
Weak		3	12	15 (21)
Universities		4	1	5 (100)
Strong		1		1 (20)
Middle		3	1	4 (80)
Weak				
Comprehensive universities and colleges		15	1	16 (100)
Strong				0 (0)
Middle		15		15 (94)
Weak			1	1 (6)
Liberal arts colleges I		10	6	16 (100)
Strong		4		4 (25)
Middle		6	4	10 (62)
Weak			2	2 (13)

Table 50. *(continued)*

Group, type of institution, and current condition	Recent trend in condition						
	Gaining ground		*Holding steady*		*Losing ground*	*Total*	
Liberal arts colleges II			24		10	34	(100)
Strong							
Middle			21		1	22	(65)
Weak			3		9	12	(35)
All responding institutions:	6	(4)	118	(69)	47 (27)	171	(100)
Strong			10			10	(6)
Middle	5		103		22	130	(76)
Weak	1		5		25	31	(18)

Source: Carnegie Council survey.

report (Minter and Bowen, 1977, p. 58). We show a slightly larger percentage of institutions overall in a weak position (18 percent), compared with their results (14 percent). On the other hand, our results indicate a somewhat smaller percentage losing ground (27 percent, compared with 32 percent). These differences must be considered minor.

A significant point of agreement, also, is the indication from our data, as from the Bowen-Minter data, that institutions in financial difficulty frequently manage to improve their positions as they make special efforts to do so.

What were the characteristics of institutions in a weak position? Nearly all were losing enrollment. This, of course, was one of our criteria for classifying an institutions as weak, but enrollment losses alone in the absence of some indication of financial weakness did not result in a classification as a weak institution. In fact, we did not find that there was a consistent relationship between enrollment losses and deficit operating balances, for example. Some institutions with enrollment losses were managing to maintain a reasonably sound financial position. Nevertheless, most of the institutions in a weak financial

position were experiencing enrollment losses. And these losses
tended to be somewhat more severe in Group I than in Group II
states (Table 51), a finding that is consistent with our conclusion
in Technical Supplement A that states with relatively large losses
in the private share of enrollment in universities and four-year
colleges were especially likely to have substantial programs of
assistance to private institutions.

The large average operating deficits shown by our weak
institutions are, of course, to be expected, because this was one of
our criteria for identifying a weak institution. However, student-
aid deficits were only slightly larger in Group I states, and were in
fact slightly smaller in Group II states, in the weak institutions
than in all respondent institutions (compare the data in Table 51
with the data in Table 49). Thus, it cannnot be said that student-
aid deficits were a major factor in explaining the generally weak
positions of these institutions, although there were a few in a
particularly serious financial condition that had exceptionally
large student-aid deficits. Interestingly enough, also, student-aid
deficits were very small or nonexistent in a number of the weak
Liberal Arts Colleges II in Group II states, suggesting that budgets
were so tight that no funds could be spared for student aid from
funds not received for this purpose.

Not all of our weak institutions were characterized as in
"serious distress" by their chief financial officers, but all institutions so characterized have been classified as weak. They
accounted for a somewhat larger percentage of weak institutions in
Group I than in Group II states.

About two-thirds of the weak institutions in both Group I and
Group II states were either under religious control or clearly had a
religious association. Catholic institutions accounted for slightly
more of these institutions in Group I states and protestant institutions in Group II states, but this difference is scarcely surprising in
view of the fact that so many of our Group II states were in the South,
where protestant institutions are particularly common. The indication that a sizable proportion of the weak institutions had religious
affiliations is consistent with our findings with respect to "losers" in
Technical Supplement A, as is the fact that significant percentages
of the weak institutions were women's colleges and that about one-
third in both groups of states were in small communities.

Table 51. Selected characteristics of institutions in relative financial difficulty in 1975-76, by type, Group I and Group II States

Group and type	Number of respondents	Percent in difficulty[a]	Average enrollment change, 1970 to 1976	Average deficit per FTE, 1974-75 to 1976-77	Percent in small communities	Average student-aid deficit per FTE, 1975-76	Percent in "serious distress"[a]	Control[b]	Percent women's colleges
Group I:	100	16%	−15.1	−376	31%	−293	38%	C 38% Pr 31%	25%
Liberal arts colleges I	31	19	−18.9	−353	50	−317	50	C 0 Pr 33	17
Liberal arts colleges II	36	22	−26.4	−445	25	−268	25	C 38 Pr 25	38
Group II:	70	21	−9.9	−404	33	−170	29	C 27 Pr 40	13
Liberal arts colleges I	15	13	−23.7	−352	0	−251	0	C 50 Pr 50	50
Liberal arts colleges II	34	35	−10.6	−445	42	−152	27	C 17 Pr 42	8

[a] Separate data are not shown for universities and comprehensive universities and colleges, in which very few were classified as weak.

[b] C = Catholic; Pr = Protestant; several institutions, with names clearly suggesting a Catholic association, have been treated as Catholic, even though officially classified as independent nonprofit by NCES.

Source: Carnegie Council survey.

Conclusions

1. The higher percentage of institutions in a weak position, especially among less selective liberal arts colleges, in Group II states suggests that state aid to private higher education is assisting private institutions in maintaining a reasonably satisfactory financial position in states where such aid is substantial.

2. On the whole, our assessment of the proportion of institutions in trouble does not differ appreciably from the Bowen-Minter findings.

3. The percentage of institutions in financial difficulty may well grow as the size of the college-age population declines. Thus, whereas we found in Technical Supplement A that institutions that actually closed between 1970 and 1975 tended to be small, marginal colleges, *and* whereas Bowen and Minter point to the fact that no institution has closed since they began their studies, we believe that closures in the 1980s may be less confined to marginal institutions.

4. To the extent that institutions are in trouble, they are predominantly in the liberal arts group—among four-year institutions, that is. Furthermore, our data show rather more substantial deterioration recently in the financial position of the more selective liberal arts collges than might have been expected. The future of some of these colleges may be rather precarious, despite the relatively strong position of many of them.

5. The changes in the financial position of private instituions from 1970–71 to 1976–77 were clearly influenced by changes in the rate of inflation. This does not mean, however, that if the inflation rate is held down in the future, all will be well. Many of the institutions that are in trouble, especially in Group I states, have been experiencing enrollment losses, and their financial difficulties appear to be associated with their enrollment problems. The proportion experiencing enrollment declines is likely to increase in the future, even though some institutions will continue to enjoy rising enrollment, especially those that cater to adults. And student-aid deficits continue to be a problem.

References

"Alaska Aid to Church Colleges Banned." *Higher Education Daily,* June 29, 1976, p. 4.

American Council on Education. *The American Freshman: National Norms for Fall.* 1967 through 1976. Title varies. Washington, D.C.: American Council on Education, annual.

American Council on Education. *A Fact Book on Higher Education: Enrollment Data.* Washington, D.C.: American Council on Education, 1973.

American Institute of Certified Public Accountants. *Industry Audit Guide, Audits of Colleges and Universities.* New York: American Institute of Certified Public Accountants, 1973.

Anderson, R. E. "The Paradox of Pluralism." *Change,* May 1977, *9* (5), 50–51.

Association of Independent Colleges and Universities of Ohio. *Toward an Effective Utilization of Independent Colleges and Universities by the State of Ohio.* Columbus: Association of Independent Colleges and Universities of Ohio, 1971.

Astin, A., King, M. R., and Richardson, G. T. *The American Freshman: National Norms for Fall 1976.* Los Angeles: Cooperative Institutional Research Program, UCLA Graduate School of Education, 1975.

Atelsek, F. J., and Gomberg, I. L. *Student Assistance: Participants and Programs, 1974–75.* Washington, D.C.: American Council on Education, 1975.

Bowen, H. R., and Minter, W. J. *Private Higher Education: First Annual Report on Financial and Educational Trends in the Private Sector of American Higher Education, 1975.* Washington, D.C.: Association of American Colleges, 1975.

Bowen, H. R., and Minter, W. J. *Private Higher Education: Second Annual Report on Financial and Educational Trends in the Private Sector of American Higher Education, 1976.* Washington, D.C.: Association of American Colleges, 1976.

Boyd, J. D. *Report on State Scholarship Programs.* Title varies. Deerfield, Ill.: Illinois State Scholarship Commission, annual.

Boyd, J. D. *State/Territory Funded Scholarship/Grant Programs to Undergraduate Students with Financial Need to Attend Public or Private Post-Secondary Educational Institutions.* National Association of State Scholarship and Grant Programs. 7th annual survey. Deerfield, Ill.: Illinois State Scholarship Commission, 1975.

Boyd, J. D. *State/Territory Funded Scholarship/Grant Programs to Undergraduate Students with Financial Need to Attend Public or Private Post-Secondary Educational Institutions.* National Association of State Scholarship and Grant Programs. 8th annual survey. Deerfield, Ill.: Illinois State Scholarship Commission, 1977.

Breneman, D., and Finn, C. (Eds.) *Public Policy and Private Higher Education* Washington, D.C.: The Brookings Institution, forthcoming.

"Budget Resolutions Cleared with Authority for Tuition Tax Credits." *Higher Education Daily*, Sept. 12, 1977, p. 1.

Carnegie Commission on Higher Education. *New Students and New Places: Policies for the Future Growth and Development of American Higher Education.* New York: McGraw-Hill, 1971.

Carnegie Commission on Higher Education. *A Classification of Institutions of Higher Education.* Berkeley, Calif.: Carnegie Commission on Higher Education, 1973a.

Carnegie Commission on Higher Education. *Higher Education: Who Pays? Who Benefits? Who Should Pay?* New York: McGraw-Hill, 1973b.

Carnegie Council on Policy Studies in Higher Education. *Low or No Tuition: The Feasibility of a National Policy for the First Two Years of College.* San Francisco: Jossey-Bass, 1975a.

Carnegie Council on Policy Studies in Higher Education. *Making Affirmative Action Work in Higher Education: An Analysis of Institutional and Federal Policies with Recommendations.* San Francisco: Jossey-Bass, 1975b.

Carnegie Council on Policy Studies in Higher Education. *The Federal Role in Postsecondary Education: Unfinished Business, 1975-1980.* San Francisco: Jossey-Bass, 1975c.

Carnegie Council on Policy Studies in Higher Education. *Progress and Problems in Medical and Dental Education: Federal Support Versus Federal Control.* San Francisco: Jossey-Bass, 1976.

Carnegie Foundation for the Advancement of Teaching, The. *More than Survival: Prospects for Higher Education in a Period of Uncertainty.* San Francisco: Jossey-Bass, 1975.

Carnegie Foundation for the Advancement of Teaching, The. *The States and Higher Education: A Proud Past and a Vital Future.* San Francisco: Jossey-Bass, 1976.

"The Cartter Report on the Leading Schools of Education, Law, and Business." *Change*, 1977, *9* (2), 44-48.

Cheit, E. F. *The New Depression in Higher Education.* New York: McGraw-Hill, 1971.

Cheit, E. F., and Lobman, T. E. *Private Philosophy and Higher Education.* Washington, D.C.: Commission on Private Philanthropy and Public Needs (Filer Commission), forthcoming.

"Conferees Agree to $1,600 Maximum on BEOG, Expanded Eligibility." *Higher Education Daily*, July 21, 1977, pp. 1-2.

Congressional Budget Office. *Postsecondary Education: The Current Federal Role and Alternative Approaches.* Washington, D.C.: U.S. Government Printing Office, 1977.

Consortium on the Financing of Higher Education. *Federal Student Assistance: A Review of Title IV of the Higher Education Act.* Hanover, N.H.: Consortium on the Financing of Higher Education, 1975.

Davis, J. S., and Kirschner, A. H. *The Ways and Means: A Study of the Needs and Resources of Students in United Negro College Fund Member Institutions.* Research Report, vol. 11, no. 1. New York: United Negro College Fund, 1977.

Education Commission of the States. "Reports on State Aid to Private Higher Education." Title varies. In *Higher Education in the States,* annual.

Education Commission of the States. "Educational Opportunity: The States and Private Higher Education." *Higher Education in the States*, 1976a, 5, 121–148.

Education Commission of the States. *State Postsecondary Education Profiles Handbook*. Report no. 88. Denver, Colo.: Education Commission of the States, 1976b.

Education Commission of the States. *State Policy and Independent Higher Education: A Report of the Task Force on State Policy and Independent Higher Education*. Denver, Colo.: Education Commission of the States, 1977.

Goldberg, D., and Anderson, A. *Projections of Population and College Enrollment in Michigan, 1970–2000*. Lansing, Mich.: Governor's Commission on Higher Education, 1974.

Harris, S. E. *Economics of Harvard*. New York: McGraw-Hill, 1970.

Hartman, R. W. "The National Bank Approach to Solutions." In L. D. Rice (Ed.), *Student Loans: Problems and Policy Alternatives*. New York: College Entrance Examination Board, 1977.

Jacobson, R. L. "Enrollment of Veterans Nosedived This Fall." *Chronicle of Higher Education*, Oct. 18, 1976, 15, (7), 1.

Jellema, W. *The Red and the Black*. Washington, D.C.: Association of American Colleges, 1971.

Jellema, W. *From Red to Black?: The Financial Status of Private Colleges and Universities*. San Francisco: Jossey-Bass, 1973.

Jenny, H., and Wynn, G. R. *The Golden Years*. Wooster, Ohio: College of Wooster Press, 1970.

McFarlane, W. H., Howard, A. E. D., and Chronister, J. L. *State Financial Measures Involving the Private Sector of Higher Education*. Washington, D.C.: National Council of Independent Colleges and Universities, 1974.

McGrath, E. J., and Neese, R. C. *Are the Church-Related Colleges Losing Students?* Tucson, Ariz.: Center for the Study of Liberal Education, University of Arizona, 1976. (Mimeographed.)

Minter, W. J., and Bowen, H. R. *Private Higher Education: Third Annual Report on Financial and Educational Trends in the Private Sector of American Higher Education, 1977*. Washington, D.C.: Association of American Colleges, 1977.

Minter, W. H., and Fadil, V. *Fall 1977 Anticipated Enrollment at Independent Colleges and Universities*. Washington, D.C.: National Association of Independent Colleges and Universities, 1977. (Mimeographed.)

National Academy of Sciences. *Membership, July 1, 1975*. Washington, D.C.: National Academy of Sciences, n.d.

Nelson, S. C. "Trends and Issues in the Financing of Private Higher Education." In D. Breneman and C. Finn (Eds.), *Public Policy and Private Higher Education*. Washington, D.C.: The Brookings Institution, forthcoming.

New Jersey Commission on Financing Post-Secondary Education. Edward E. Booher, Chairman. *Financing in an Era of Uncertainty*. Draft Commission Report. Princeton: New Jersey Commisssion on Financing Post-Secondary Education, 1976. (Mimeographed.)

New York State Board of Regents. Nathan M. Pusey, Chairman. *Report of the Regents Advisory Commission on the Financial Problems of Postsecondary Institutions*. Albany: New York State Board of Regents, 1975.

The President. *Economic Report of the President, 1977*. Washington, D.C.: U.S. Government Printing Office, 1977.

Riesman, D. "The Future of Diversity in a Time of Retrenchment." *Higher*

Education, 1975, *4,* 461–482.

Roose, K. D., and Andersen, C. J. *A Rating of Graduate Programs.* Washington, D.C.: American Council on Education, 1970.

Rudolph, F. *The American College and University: A History.* New York: Knopf, 1962.

Sack, S. *History of Higher Education in Pennsylvania.* Harrisburg: Pennsylvania Historical and Museum Commission, 1963.

Smith, P., and Henderson, C. *A Financial Taxonomy of Institutions of Higher Education.* Washington, D.C.: American Council on Education, 1976.

Smith, P., and Henderson, C. *Federal Student Aid: Who Receives It and How Is It Packaged?* Washington, D.C.: American Council on Education, 1977.

Special Analyses: Budget of the United States Government, Fiscal Year, 1978. Washington, D.C.: U.S. Government Printing Office, 1977.

Spence, D. S. *A Profile of Higher Education in the South in 1985.* Atlanta, Ga.: Southern Regional Education Board, 1977.

"SSIG Goes Nationwide with $60 Million in Grants." *Higher Education Daily,* July 15, 1977, p. 5.

Sunley, E. M., Jr. "Federal and State Tax Policies." In D. Breneman and C. Finn (Eds.), *Public Policy and Private Higher Education.* Washington, D.C.: The Brookings Institution, forthcoming.

U.S. Bureau of the Census. "Population Estimates and Projections." *Current Population Reports,* ser. P-25, no. 311. Washington, D.C.: U.S. Government Printing Office, 1965.

U.S. Bureau of the Census. "School Enrollment." *Current Population Reports,* ser. P-20, no. 190. Washington, D.C.: U.S. Government Printing Office, 1969.

U.S. Bureau of the Census. "School Enrollment." *Current Population Reports,* ser. P-20, no. 222. Washington, D.C.: U.S. Government Printing Office, 1971.

U.S. Bureau of the Census. *1972 Census of the Government, vol. 11, Part 1, Taxable and Other Property Values.* Washington, D.C.: U.S. Government Printing Office, 1973.

U.S. Bureau of the Census. "Population Estimates and Projections." *Current Population Reports,* ser. P-25, no. 519. Washington, D.C.: U.S. Government Printing Office, 1974a.

U.S. Bureau of the Census. "School Enrollment." *Current Population Reports,* ser.P-20, no. 260. Washington, D.C.: U.S. Government Printing Office, 1974b.

U.S.Bureau of the Census. "Population Estimates and Projections." *Current Population Reports,* ser. P-25, no. 601. Washington, D.C.: U.S. Government Printing Office, 1975.

U.S. Bureau of the Census. "Population Estimates and Projections." *Current Population Reports,* ser. P-25, no. 614, Washington, D.C.: U.S. Government Printing Office, 1976a.

U.S. Bureau of the Census. "School Enrollment." *Current Population Reports,* ser. P-20, no. 303. Washington, D.C.: U.S. Government Printing Office, 1976b.

U.S. Department of Defense. OASD (Comptroller), Directorate for Information Operations. *Selected Manpower Statistics.* Washington, D.C.: U.S. Government Printing Office, 1974.

U.S. Department of Health, Education and Welfare. *Financial Statistics of Institutions of Higher Education: Property, 1970–71 and 1971–72.* Washington, D.C.: U.S. Government Printing Office, 1974.

"U.S. Funds for Higher Education." *Chronicle of Higher Education,* July 5, 1977, *14* (17), 11.

U.S. National Center for Education Statistics. *Education Directory, 1973–74: Higher Education.* Washington, D.C.: U.S Government Printing Office, 1974a.

U.S. National Center for Education Statistics. *Financial Statistics of Institutions of Higher Education: Property, 1970–71 and 1971–72.* Washington, D.C.: U.S. Government Printing Office, 1974b.

U.S. National Center for Education Statistics. *Digest of Educational Statistics, 1974.* Washington, D.C.: U.S. Government Printing Office, 1975.

U.S. National Center for Education Statistics. *Higher Education: Education Directory, 1975–76.* Washington, D.C.: U.S. Government Printing Office, 1976.

U.S. National Center for Education Statistics. *Digest of Educational Statistics, 1976 Edition.* Washington, D.C.: U.S. Government Printing Office, 1977a.

U.S. National Center for Education Statistics. *Education Directory, Colleges and Universities, 1976–77.* Washington, D.C.: U.S. Government Printing Office, 1977b.

U.S. National Center for Education Statistics. *Prepublication Tables on Fall 1976 Enrollment.* Washington, D.C.: U.S. Government Printing Office, Feb. 3, 1977c.

U.S. National Center for Education Statistics. *Projections of Education Statistics to 1985–86.* Washington, D.C.: U.S. Government Printing Office, 1977d.

U.S. Office for Civil Rights. *Racial and Ethnic Enrollment Data from Institutions of Higher Education, Fall 1974.* Washington, D.C.: U.S. Government Printing Office, 1976.

U.S. Office of Education. *Biennial Survey of Education in the United States.* Selected Issues. Washington, D.C.: U.S. Government Printing Office, 1932, 1944, and 1952.

Whitehead, J.S. *The Separation of College and State: Columbia, Dartmouth and Yale, 1776–1876.* New Haven, Conn.: Yale University Press, 1973.

Index